Sacred Geometry
Tarot deck

inner space

About inner.space

inner.space is an innovative platform for spiritual development with next level meditations based on sacred geometry and cosmic sounds. Ancient wisdom and new technology come together in the form of simple tools and techniques that facilitate your personal growth.

inner.space offers guided meditations, workshops and items that can contribute to refining your perception and expanding your consciousness.

Tune in to your natural state of being.
Let a new world emerge from within.
A life with less ego and more love begins with exploring the space within yourself.

inner.space invites all searchers to go within.
The only way out is in.

www.inner.space

Table of contents

How do you use the inner.space Sacred Geometry Tarot deck?

The Sacred Geometry Tarot deck is a new interpretation of the classic tarot. The symbols have been replaced by meditative geometric figures. The cards are divided into six series, each with its own life theme.

The first series includes all of the major life experiences. The other five series are about events in the areas of personal development, creativity, wisdom, love and consciousness.

Each card bears a geometric image, a title and a reference to a Platonic body. All three have their own meaning:

— The geometric image has a meditative function. You can use the card in a spread, and also put it on your altar or bedside table for a while to activate your intention.

— The title refers to the interpretation in the booklet.

— The platonic bodies refer to the six basic forms that make up the geometric images. Each form has its own possibilities and properties.

The cards and the interpretations are intended for the purposes of contemplation and the activation of your higher intentions. You can draw individual cards, use them in a spread, or mix the cards with other decks.

However you use the cards, the inner.space Sacred Geometry Tarot deck is intended as a means of transcending your experiences. Life is seen as a game to reach a freer way of looking, thinking and experiencing.

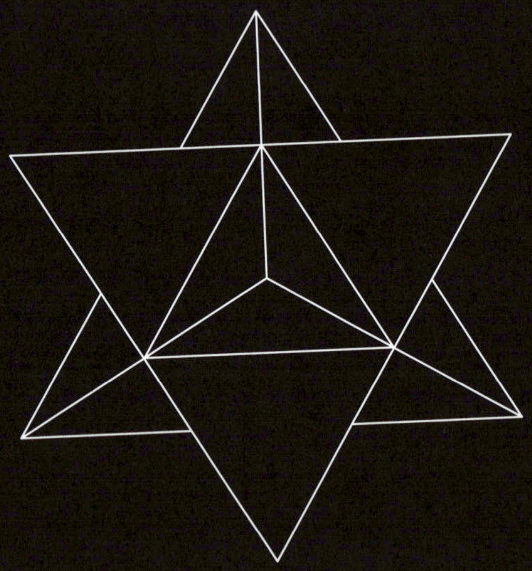

Star tetrahedron series I – XXII

The life cycle

In this card deck, the Star Tetrahedron series stands for the life cycle; the progression from 'ignorance' to 'the wisdom of not knowing'. Experiences of separateness are invitations to spiritual growth. Duality is a product of our thinking, not of life itself (which simply 'is'). The Star Tetrahedron series offers you the opportunity to see through the illusions of your experiences and your thoughts, in order to achieve a broader consciousness.

Harmony

The evolution from individual to collective. When you want a world that's less about 'I' and more about 'we', this requires a shift in yourself. Harmony also stands for connecting worlds and developing empathic abilities. It's about feeling more love for more people, as if your heart is growing.

Meaning in combination with the star tetrahedron

When you no longer feel you need to defend yourself, you can be in the world just as you are. You can view the other and the possible judgment of the other from a broader awareness. All of the experiences that life offers are an invitation to explore: what can I learn from this, what can I leave with the other (or take with me), and what is my contribution to the whole?

Limitlessness

Speaking your truth to others from your heart returns you to the right perspective – that is, a higher perspective. Seek and gather the courage to go beyond the boundaries of fear, shame and limitation.

Meaning in combination with the star tetrahedron

When you leave behind the 'must and want', you can start living more from within, free of your mental beliefs and emotional tendencies. It's no longer about what you must and want, but about what comes from within. Free thinking does not arise from reason (head) or emotion (belly), but from the heart, where unconditionality resides. Observing from the heart (the 'heartmind') can bring wonderful new ideas and show limitless possibilities.

Inner voice

Recognizing your true inner voice. The voice of the heart is greater than your own personal interest, and it invites you to grow.

Meaning in combination with the star tetrahedron

Intuition is not the same as emotion. Emotion is subject to the survival mechanism of the ego. Intuition is the voice of the heart. You'll be able to better distinguish this voice from all the other voices in your head by entering seclusion. It's only by withdrawing from the commotion of life that you can hear it and understand its message.

Initiation

If you can see your own movements as a run-up to a greater change, this phase of life becomes a form of training; preparation for that greater leap, an initiation into the future.

Meaning in combination with the star tetrahedron

Sometimes it's necessary to give into your urges in order to find out what you truly long for. Sometimes you have to 'cut loose' in order to see yourself clearly, and to see that what you really want is not about gaining worldly possessions and temporary pleasure (although you don't have to condemn this either). Use your senses in a more subtle way to turn inwards.

Christ consciousness

When karma's gestation period comes to an end, every human being can be reborn. A conscious state of being is who you really are: not you as an individual, but that which observes everything without judgment. This 'being' is your real self. This form of consciousness is like crystal: pure, clear and translucent.

Meaning in combination with the star tetrahedron

Seeing through the illusion of something you believed in can feel like dying. Yet it is precisely this surrender that is needed to receive the light from which a new consciousness emerges.

Mastery

It's only when you give up the 'need to know' that you can truly receive and live in a more effortless way, free and trusting. You no longer need to know, but can simply live by being allowed to be, and growing by embracing all experiences: this is mastery.

Meaning in combination with the star tetrahedron

You are free of fear when you know that you don't have to be able to trust the other, but can trust your higher self from a place of release. Nothing is needed if you dare to live from the truth of the present. Self-esteem is nothing more nor less than feeling your own power.

Reunification

This is about being able to see meeting the other as meeting a soul mate. What can you learn from the other, from the dynamic between you? The intention is to connect, without judgment and from a perspective of curiosity.

Meaning in combination with the star tetrahedron

Entering into relationships, really committing to the other, is choosing to unmask yourself. All of the challenges that a relationship brings invite you to explore questions such as: when am I really myself, and when am I hiding behind my opinions and beliefs, my fears and emotions?

Transcendence

Whenever you set out to achieve something, you'll find all kinds of ifs and buts coming up in you that you elevate to the status of truths, without ever having experienced whether they really are. By taking continued, very small steps, you'll move away from 'yes, but what if…' thinking towards new experiences, which will show you that life can sometimes be very different to what your thoughts sometimes lead you to believe.

Meaning in combination with the star tetrahedron

When you get closer to realization by taking small steps, your focus becomes stronger and your courage greater. Then comes the point where you no longer allow yourself to be distracted by the ego, but lead your life from a higher purpose.

Self-love

Unconditional love is free of expectations or ideals. It is a fulfilled state of being: in this state nothing needs to change, there is a complete acceptance of how things are. The question to be explored is: how can you be alone in love? Self-love may well be an exercise in 'being'. Feeling that you are there, without judgment.

Meaning in combination with the star tetrahedron

Primal energy is sometimes needed to help you access the fire of your own self-love. Any form of yelling or screaming aloud can help you to get there.

Commitment

There's an idea out there that you have to be good enough, you have to adapt, you have to solve things for someone else. You can transcend this by turning the focus onto yourself. You learn to be committed to yourself by seeing and honoring what you do here on Earth.

Meaning in combination with the star tetrahedron

Give yourself time to do nothing, to incubate. Underground growth is necessary before you can come into bloom. Come to see that wisdom is not about 'you should know', but instead is always about 'you can keep learning'. This is how you develop leadership with respect to your own life.

Abundance

Scarcity is a belief. We live on a self-sufficient spaceship. Fear and greed drive the unfair distribution of resources. When we make an inner shift from 'fear of deprivation' to 'relying on our own abundance', we can create wealth ourselves and share it with others.

Meaning in combination with the star tetrahedron

You can't control exactly what form abundance will take. You can attract abundance by giving abundantly that which overflows in you. Because you have so much of it, you don't need anything in return. This is the basic attitude for creating abundance in your life.

Resonance

Developing an awareness of 'what am I sending out and what am I allowing in?' clarifies your capacity to send and receive. You can send and receive static, or you can consciously choose to tune in to a particular program to find resonance in what you hear and say.

Meaning in combination with the star tetrahedron

When seeking resonance, however, it's also important to allow space for multiple voices. You don't have to agree with everyone or share the same opinion. Being open and fluid is often more valuable than holding on to an opinion.

Reconsideration

Reconsider previous decisions. Dare to doubt, release a previously held opinion that no longer feels true. Listening to what's true now means you can take new steps in a fresh direction.

Meaning in combination with the star tetrahedron

The road doesn't come to an end if you release an old opinion. Find peace in accepting that you've changed your mind. Maintain this position for a while, as if it were a yoga exercise. Releasing what no longer works opens up the way to a new beginning.

Unfolding

Waiting does not have to be negative. It can mean that you're laying the last of the foundations for an inner construction project that's been under way for quite some time. Be patient and don't cut off this process. Your life may take a natural turn that enables your new reality to unfold automatically.

Meaning in combination with the star tetrahedron

During unfolding, you may sometimes fear giving up an aspect of your personality. 'If I give up my familiar behavior, I'll lose control of my life.' However, this mourning process is actually announcing the arrival of something new.

Ascension

This is about taking leadership over your own life. You don't have to achieve or pursue anything, or follow something or someone. Your spiritual path is personal and inimitable. No one can impose it on you, and you cannot impose it on anyone else. Investigate and follow your own truth, and do not try to convert others.

Meaning in combination with the star tetrahedron

When you feel secure, inner desire can work in a healthy way: you are simultaneously self-confident and selfless in your actions. This allows you to rise above the ego and discover what spiritual leadership really is.

Unmasking

What does being 'real' mean? Who are you without your opinions, preoccupations, preferences, stories and the 'truths' you've told about yourself so often? By simply being present – without taking a position or striving to do your best – you are more authentic, more in the now and more openly connected with the other. To be without masks is to see, show and embrace all of your qualities without identification.

Meaning in combination with the star tetrahedron

By seeing the roles that you sometimes play, you can see for yourself what's not true. You can also pierce the illusions in the outside world if you start seeing experiences as scenes. You can look at your life and ask yourself: what does this moment symbolize? What is happening here? Break free of identification and see what you can learn.

Reforming

You have created a reality that works more against you than for you. The system of rules, agreements and convictons you're holding onto no longer resonates with who you are and where you want to go. You can see that you've locked yourself into a matrix of solidified beliefs, an outdated system that requires reform. Dare to leave behind your own dogmas and old truths, so you can start experimenting again.

Meaning in combination with the star tetrahedron

A rough time or an emotionally turbulent period can lead to an eruption. This may seem disastrous at the time, but later you'll be able to look back on it with a great sense of gratitude.

The life cycle XVII

Osmosis

With judgments, blame and convictions, you keep the other at a distance. Look beyond the duality to the underlying process. You'll be able to see where both parties mirror each other: they each lack the thing that makes the other strong. You obtain this power through osmosis; the blending of worlds, from which a new world of experience arises. Be inspired by the power of the other. Don't keep your own strength to yourself.

Meaning in combination with the star tetrahedron

Harmony is to be found in gentleness and humility. By making yourself visible, without pretensions, but by being clear, you will allow others to see your true powers. This will enable your specific abilities to be recognized for what they are, and you'll be able to merge with a new world in which you can give the very best of yourself.

Transition

A transition can be very frightening, because it brings up things like: 'What exactly will the new situation look like?! What's going to happen to me?!' Admitting that you cannot know this and then surrendering to the unknown can make you feel insecure. But it's precisely the 'being uncertain' that gives you the openness you need to learn from your new experiences instead of reacting from a place of resistance. Uncertainty is the birthplace of curiosity.

Meaning in combination with the star tetrahedron

If you're going through a transition, certain experiences can feel overwhelming and incomprehensible. Sometimes there is no other option than to let yourself be swept up and carried along on the wild waters of the experience. Once the storm subsides and you've come through the stormy hours of the night, you can rest. Everything that's been shaken up so wildly can now come to rest once more. The previously muddy waters will become clear again.

Development

By continually adapting to your environment and reacting to circumstances, you can lose the feeling that you're leading a life of your own. Instead of turning the wheel of life yourself, you're walking around in circles inside a treadmill. You can only develop yourself further by coming to creativity from within. The other option is reactivity. Turn the wheel yourself, and turn the treadmill into an upward spiral.

Meaning in combination with the star tetrahedron

When you step out of the treadmill, the scales will fall from your eyes. At first, everything will still be uncertain, and it'll all come down to persistence and perseverance. Trust will follow. Having a new perspective changes everything that you see. That sounds light, and it is Light. You can now see with God's eyes. You'll illuminate your life with your own inner light, and you'll now be able to see for yourself that all is love.

Calling

Activate and accelerate. This is your moment. Where you once were caught up in thinking and doubting, now the impulse is so strong that everything simply says: go for it! Are you right, or will you regret this? There is no such thing as a good choice; the outcome is not fixed in advance. Sometimes, the alarm clock simply goes off, and it's time to get up and enter into the experience.

Meaning in combination with the star tetrahedron

The decision seems to have already been made unconsciously somewhere. This calling is not about a change of circumstances, but a whole new consciousness. You are directly connected to the truth through the merging of your higher self with life's forces. Synchronicity is your compass, and everything's now a game of learning and creation.

The life cycle XXI

Unity consciousness

You can experience that you are part of a greater whole; a whole that's of a different order than worldly reality. When you're in contact with your surroundings, you experience a natural love – for other people, for nature, but also when you're alone. There is no separateness, no loneliness, no distance, no time.

Meaning in combination with the star tetrahedron

Enlightenment is no longer restricted to the realm of meditation or other ways of withdrawing into silence. Enlightenment also manifests itself out in the World. There is no longer an inside or outside. All miracles live in the world soul. Universe, body, earth, spirit are one here. This is where Everything speaks and lives.

The life cycle XXII

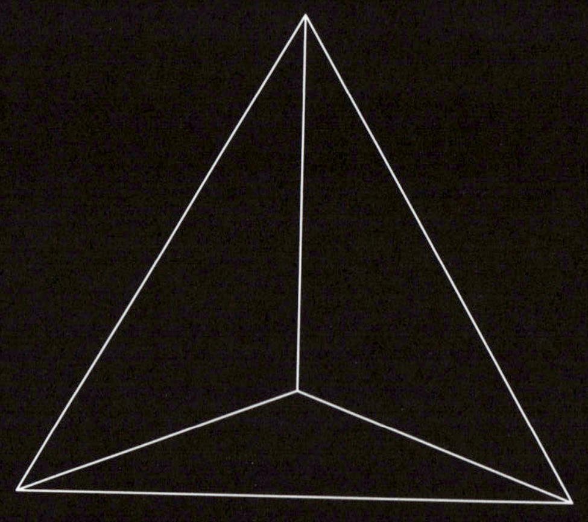

Tetrahedron series I – XIV

Growth & strength

In this card deck, the Tetrahedron series stands for life themes such as 'own power' and 'growth'. It's about exploring your specific power, determining your direction and recognizing your higher purpose. Life offers you situations that invite you to undertake creative development, train your natural strength and make your way of acting effectively visible. This series will help you learn to go your own way.

Natural time

Deadlines and full schedules may sometimes give you the feeling that our invented time is the only real time. However, you could also see it as an artificial timeline that is different from our natural rhythm. If you connect to natural time, you'll experience life less as a straight line you have to follow, and more as an infinite cycle of spiraling motion. Sometimes you climb, and sometimes you descend. This insight gives you more peace of mind when you're busy and more acceptance and calmness when things are quieter.

Meaning in combination with tetrahedron

You may have lost sight of your own natural development due to being under too much stress. By looking at your own process and recognizing a cycle in it, you'll be more able to see what you need and at what time. This will allow processes to run more smoothly, and more subtle possibilities, opportunities and solutions will become apparent.

Empowerment

On the one hand you want more freedom, and on the other hand you're afraid of the responsibilities that will go with it. Can I handle it? Am I being unrealistic about my goals? Is this really for me? It helps to accept that you're afraid. To admit your fear, is to feel your strength. If you continue to embrace your fear, hope will win automatically.

Meaning in combination with tetrahedron

Sometimes it is necessary to confront something in reality. Perhaps you'd rather avoid a discussion or argument. However, going into battle can also be a very good exercise in measuring your own strength and discovering where your power is. It's also good to dare to doubt yourself in order to find out where your attachment is. Sometimes, taking responsibility gives you exactly the freedom you're looking for.

Imprint

Your life does not follow a mapped out path; instead, it's a colorful creation made up of experiences and thoughts. It's a kind of impression of the choices you've made. Some imprints remain sharp and clear, while others fade. Life is subject to constant change. You can pick up various storylines from your past and transcend them by interpreting them in a new way. By continuously advancing in your insight, you make your past, present and future fluid.

Meaning in combination with tetrahedron

Don't look back, but look ahead instead. Continuing to analyze why and how something happened can blur your future focus. Focusing on the past won't prove you right. If you do something at a loss, or find a way to grow from it, then you can equalize it or even make it profitable for yourself. Trying to turn loss into profit makes you creative, and gives you the desire to engage in life again.

Victory

Victory is not the same as success. Achieving social success is often just as much fun, but the moment passes quickly. The process that precedes it and the insights you have gained afterwards are what deserve the prize. When something has been difficult, it's actually the great insight that is a reward for the battle you've fought.

Meaning in combination with tetrahedron

By optimizing the creative process, standing strongly in your own place and allowing others to do the things they're better at, you create space and harmony.
A process in which work is done with self-confidence, humor and personal perspective is a victory that exceeds the exaggerated importance of the end result. This can be about a work process, but also a relationship. It's not the final picture that's important; having fun together today is what it's all about.

Rescue

We cannot predict outcomes. Nor can we control the behavior of others. You can't save 'the lot' on your own. However, you can make a conscious contribution to collective processes by exploring each other's desires and boundaries openly. Take the initiative for self-reliance in relation to the other and be the first to state your own desires and boundaries.

Meaning in combination with tetrahedron

Arguments, fighting or hassle can be a good reason for practicing guarding your boundaries, taking responsibility or expressing yourself more clearly. Making mistakes yourself is sometimes necessary for clarifying what you need to learn. It's an opportunity to get to know your own ego and blind spots, even if you thought you weren't bothered by them any longer.

Growth & strength V

Transfiguration

**You are finding a new form on multiple levels.
Old patterns and negative beliefs can be discarded, and new insights can change your behavior.
Give yourself room to experiment, and permission not to have to stay who you are.**

Meaning in combination with tetrahedron

Without your old patterns, you may feel insecure and tend to postpone living your life. However, you can listen to yourself and get moving at the same time. By moving in new ways, you allow new forms to come into existence.

Perspective

It's not that your options have suddenly run out, it's more that you just can't see them any more. Perhaps you've been blinded by setbacks, and this is actually asking you to go within rather than casting about in despair. From a place of tranquility, you'll be able to open your eyes once more and really see. Instead of searching for a rational solution, or for a fix in response to your need, embark on a journey from your heart to discover what inspires you. This will remind you of how you arrive at visions and new perspectives: not by thinking, but by dreaming.

Meaning in combination with tetrahedron

By giving trust, understanding and empathy – first to yourself, then to the other – you open up the opportunity for gaining new insights and great revelations. First go inside, observe what you're experiencing, and respond only after that. This will enable you to develop a richer perspective.

Growth & strength VII

Momentum

You can get better at recognizing your own natural momentum. 'Am I ready for this? Is it perhaps okay to give myself a push? What would happen if I slept on it for a night?' By challenging yourself with these kinds of questions, you can find out whether your sense of timing is driven by ego or by your soul's desire.

Meaning in combination with tetrahedron

Perhaps you tend to give up, let the moment pass you by. But perhaps you don't have to be so rigorous. It may look like you're collapsing and can't go on, but is this really true? A brief break can provide you with clarity. Don't use the silence as an excuse for not having to do what scares you (but which you do want to do). This is a time to recharge so that you can make the most of the next moment.

Resistance

When you feel you have to do something but don't want to, then something in you is not in alignment. If you want to get past this, you can go back to simply 'being'. What is the grief beneath your resistance, and the desire beneath all the layers of emotion, drama and excuses? Trust that resistance is a signal telling you to find out what does move you.

Meaning in combination with tetrahedron

The greater the resistance, the more thorough the self-examination that is needed. Don't let the ego tell you what's going on, but keep going deeper, layer by layer. Be really honest with yourself now. What are you afraid of? What are you putting off? You need these answers in order to develop. If you use clever tricks to avoid them, you will keep encountering the same situation. If you now decide to really start investigating, do it with love and understanding for the small, frightened part of yourself. Take on the role of a coaching parent in this process.

Growth & strength IX

Repetition

The growth of awareness proceeds in cycles. Sometimes repetition is necessary. You may find yourself thinking: 'Wait a moment, I've already been here before. Haven't I worked this out already?' Still you're presented with another experience dealing with the same subject. This is a chance to clarify and resolve the minor issues that still remain. These repeat exercises quickly show you what you can use this experience for.

Meaning in combination with tetrahedron

You may find it difficult to see what you need to do when you're feeling discouraged. You won't be able to think or act strategically when you're in this mindset. What you need to do now is clean up, tackle the issues, go through it, and get yourself moving again. It's lighter than you think.

Joining

Separateness is an illusion, yet in 'reality' you may feel lonely. Sometimes you need the recognition of another person in order to be able to see yourself. Who are your heroes, which people inspire you? No matter how inaccessible some may be, there is always a way to connect so you can be inspired again and be with others in a loving way. Sometimes a new phase in life requires a new tribe.

Meaning in combination with tetrahedron

Your tastes and preferences have changed, but are not yet developed. Adapting to something you're not familiar with requires searching. If something doesn't appeal to you immediately on the first layer, it may still be worth looking deeper. Even if it turns out not to be for you, that doesn't matter so much. You're practicing your discernment and entering new worlds. This helps you get to know yourself better, and enables you to become more open, more tolerant and less rejecting towards others.

Protection

Sometimes you may be more sensitive to information from outside or someone else's energy. You can learn to filter influences more consciously without having to close yourself off completely from the outside world. You can also switch from 'receive' to 'send' mode. This helps prevent someone else's negative emotion or energy from penetrating so deeply, and you can consciously emanate your desired state of being to your surroundings.

Meaning in combination with tetrahedron

If you manifest yourself more clearly and act as the transmitter more often, you become stronger and can opt more for adventure. Setting boundaries gives you space. By living according to your own boundaries and desires, you can have more empathy for others and better align yourself with the outside world, because you no longer have to close yourself off.

Balance

You can get out of balance due to the success of others. If you feel that someone is ahead of you or is taking something away from you, you may feel jealous or dejected. Perhaps somewhere you're judging yourself for not being good enough, or you're afraid of missing out. Ideas are never unique, but your creativity is. Be inspired by what you like about someone else. This will help you to further develop your own creativity.

Meaning in combination with tetrahedron

Once you discover what your soft power is, you'll be able to cultivate new territory. You can use soft energy to inspire people instead of trying to convince them of something. You'll get more out of an open conversation than a debate. When you build on your own creativity, the other is no longer a threat, but a source of enrichment.

Growth & strength XIII

Trust

If you trust yourself, you won't be so concerned about whether or not you can trust others. In order to cultivate trust, you need to pay attention to yourself. Feeling emotions is a valuable exercise for shedding light on the unknown. A dream, feeling or inspiration is not a 'fantasy': it's a message from your subconscious that's intended to give you information about something.

Meaning in combination with tetrahedron

Idealism requires an honest investigation. Wanting to do good is much more frequently about the ego than the heart. If you can get clear on this, it won't be about what you want any more. Instead, it will become more like: how can I best expend my efforts to make my own unique contribution? Less contrived and more based on intuition, you'll dare to tackle things, nourished by a happy inner child in your heart.

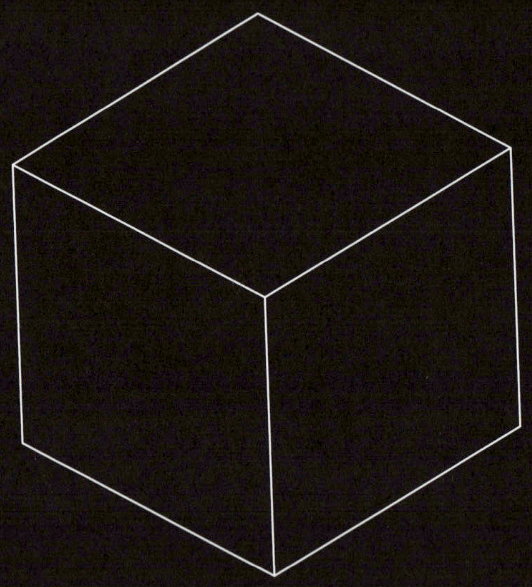

Hexahedron series I – XIV

The art of creation

In this card deck, the Hexahedron series stands for the themes of 'materialization', 'creative power' and 'sense of reality'. It's about converting your own value into added value in this world, and embodying your process. Your 'person' is the vehicle that you've been given in order to learn and create something in this life. How can you realize yourself and devote yourself to the whole?

Manifestation

Perhaps you're not so afraid that something won't work, but that it will work. 'Be careful what you wish for, because you'll get it,' says the sage who knows just how true this can be. You don't know in advance exactly what your dream will look like once it's been realized. After that experience, you'll know: once your dreams are fulfilled, they're just another new reality. People are creators; your imagination is the origin of everything you materialize.

Meaning in combination with hexahedron

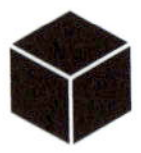

You are provided with the capacity to create. Whether and how you develop this capacity is your own responsibility. Realizing your imagination requires trust, strength and persistence. It's about saying 'yes' time and time again, and then doing it. Is this scary or difficult? Perhaps, but the fact that you can start over with realizing gives you a lot of freedom.

Perseverance

Giving up is the only reason that something definitely won't work. The point is perseverance. You really won't just break. If you're feeling like giving up, that's a good reason to check if everything is all right, and whether you're still 'on track' with your desired intention. If your answer to this is uncertain, you should re-evaluate your true intention. Perhaps your higher goal has been hacked by the ego. But if your heart shouts 'yes!', then go for it! Completing something will always take you further. It's not even really about the result, but about the practice of persevering.

Meaning in combination with hexahedron

Uncertainty makes it difficult to persevere, even when you might barely have got started. The lack of stability and experience is useful, however, because it also allows you to be flexible and playful. If you take your insecurity a little more lightly and put it to good use, you'll be able to learn a lot from it.

Transformation

Real transformation requires surrender. Without surrender, change remains superficial, cosmetic, at ego level. Trans-formation says something about 'changing shape'. When you're facing this process, it can feel like 'having to die'. But just as with reincarnation, where the changing of life is seen as putting on a new coat, here too surrender will mean a new life.

Meaning in combination with hexahedron

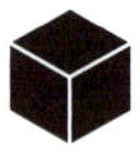

If you possess the knowledge, technique, wisdom and love for what you aspire to, then you'll have everything you need to achieve that one higher goal. Sometimes it's necessary to take a step back, to tune in on a detail that requires attention. When you shape something new, it's also good to look at how the shape arises. That is, the work is not only 'your doing', but is also something that reveals itself to you.

Processing

You may be experiencing a major leap in development; a phase in which everything seems to be speeding up. Learning is easier, and life flows more naturally. However, there may still be something that you need to process. Right now, you might not have much interest in or attention for that. Nevertheless, this is a good time to do it. During this accelerated phase, you can clean up 'residual pain' very efficiently and it can greatly clarify your vision.

Meaning in combination with hexahedron

Ignoring what you still need to process can lead to contraction. Vigor can turn into inner turmoil and the urge to control things. Take the time to look at what's bothering you. Examining this is already part of the healing process.

Self-confidence

Self-confidence is something the ego likes to make use of, saying things like 'I'm so insecure' or 'I'm self-confident'. Self-confidence has nothing to do with being certain, because certainty is an illusion anyway. The only thing we know for sure is that everything is changeable and impermanent.
Trust is not the same as certainty. We often project 'trust' onto something or someone else: can I trust you? The true question is more: 'How can I be true to myself in this connection or this situation?'

Meaning in combination with hexahedron

Asking for help can be exactly what you need to become stronger. Underlying the act of asking for help is the insight that self-confidence is completely different to believing that you have to be able to do everything alone. Seeking to connect from a position of vulnerability helps you to develop your own strength. Please note: this exercise is not about getting guaranteed support, but about asking for help. No matter what the answer is, the act of asking will always help you to grow.

Direction

'Choosing a direction' is not an intellectual matter. It can be helpful to think strategically, but this provides no guarantees. Navigating on the basis of resonance is another way of choosing your direction. It requires a connection with your foundation and your higher self. By continually alternating between grounding yourself and broadening your gaze, you can determine your course with awareness. This vertical alignment helps you to choose your path in a less intellectual, less reactive way.

Meaning in combination with hexahedron

Refining your vision with respect to others can be helpful. Without allowing yourself to be influenced too much, testing your vision can contribute to gaining a clearer idea of where you want to go. Talking to people outside your culture or comfort zone can be very refreshing and inspiring. It can help you to release beliefs that you didn't realize you had, making your path even freer.

Resilience

A phase of strong growth brings new experiences through which you learn a lot, become stronger, and can give yourself direction. It can feel as if you're outgrowing your surroundings, but perhaps you're the one who's most bothered by that. It's not so important. During these accelerated growth phases, it's good to feel how resilient you are. If you make a mistake or fall back into old behavior briefly, you'll pick yourself up quickly again and carry on. You're more quick to forgive yourself when you're open and willing to learn. This lightness enables you to make short work of all your resistance.

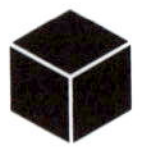

Meaning in combination with hexahedron

If you're in acceleration mode yourself, you may become impatient. Maintaining lightness at those moments when you have to wait a little is an act of patience. It's almost impossible to achieve something by forcing it. Too much pressure is brought to bear on it, and it loses the resilience it needs. If you can relax while waiting at the traffic lights, you'll be able to get under way again smoothly in due course.

Focus

Is your lens focused? Or is your goal too indistinct? If you're well-focused, you won't have to keep questioning your goal or your motivation. What you need is good visibility and a firm tread. Take some time to think about where you might need to sharpen your focus, and alternate your gaze between the distant destination and your next step.

Meaning in combination with hexahedron

If you can look at yourself in a loving way, you will also see that you create your own good fortune. What do you need to stay dedicated to your work now? No distractions, the right tools and good self-care. By taking this approach, you can turn a favorite activity into a fully-fledged craft. Self-esteem precedes this.

Coming home

You don't need to travel any distance at all in order to come home. Home is here and now. However, you may feel that you're a long way from yourself. Perhaps you've had to experience a lot, you've spent a considerable amount of time around people, or you've been thinking deeply about things. To come back to yourself, you need to let your mind rest in your heart, surrendering thought to love. Fill yourself with peaceful emptiness and comfort yourself: home is where you are now; you can always be here.

Meaning in combination with hexahedron

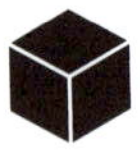

When you're absolutely home, the way you value moments changes. Relaxation and a feeling of satisfaction do not make things more boring: instead, you become more sensitive and less consumptive. Suddenly you'll be able to experience beauty in small moments without having to devour them. Valuing is much more about honoring what is there, by means of a much more subtle form of perception.

Breakthrough

A breakthrough is both powerful and unsustainable. The powers brought to bear in this process are not yours alone. The art is to work together with nature and your circumstances.

Meaning in combination with hexahedron

A need for stability. Strengthening your foundations. Know your places of power and make sure you can be there a lot. Find the people who help you return to your core. Seek solidity so you can recharge yourself during this calm before the storm.

Opportunities

If you think that opportunities come from outside, it may be that every opportunity brings a limitation with it. In 'if and then' thinking, opportunities depend on circumstances. Opportunities remain conditional if you place them outside yourself. You create opportunities through your own looking and thinking. Examine how you direct your thoughts. Do you respond to fearful thoughts, or do you consciously set an intention?

Meaning in combination with hexahedron

Once you see opportunities again, you may become a bit jumpy and reactive. Your ideas are still young and undeveloped. A certain dedication is needed, and learning and honoring. This will transform reactivity into attentiveness. Practicing gratitude helps with this.

Completeness

Spiritual growth is not about becoming a good person. You don't have to become better than you are. Spiritual growth is not linear, it's about opening up and out. It's about expanding your perception so you can see and embrace every aspect of yourself. It's about being free enough to see that no matter how vast your perspective, you'll still always be limited. Nothing or no one possesses the whole truth. Being able to recognize your incompleteness is perhaps the closest you can get to being complete.

Meaning in combination with hexahedron

Now that you've seen the big picture, including the limitations, you can release the power to get something good off the ground. Accepting the idea of being both part & whole, and being able to see this in everything and everyone, frees you from the notion that we should all think the same way or that we shouldn't be different.

Emergence

Emergence requires a process of incubation. This is a time of enfolding, darkness and deep rest, before you can come out of your pupa and unfold your decorated wings, like a butterfly. This time when you appear to be doing nothing is actually when it's all happening. Emergence is also about no longer playing a role. Because no matter how beautiful the role you play may be, it is not real. The real you may be fragile - just like a butterfly -, but in that fragility is its beauty. Vulnerability also creates lightness. Fragile wings are able to take flight.

Meaning in combination with hexahedron

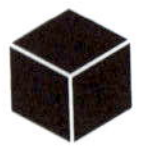

The freedom to step out of your fixed forms, patterns and thinking. Allow yourself to live it up a little with more time, space and freedom to learn to play. Dare to be a little looser, softer or more childlike, to be more free in the way you occupy space. Taking this space is essential; the feeling of being allowed to have a holiday is a true learning experience.

Knowledge

You not only have wisdom within you, but also the capacity to acquire knowledge. When you want to develop, you may feel afraid: 'I know too little, I don't have the right pieces of paper!' Sometimes it can be great to go 'back to school', to study and learn once again. Research is a natural ability, but it's also good to realize that the golden egg is not hidden in knowledge outside of you, but in your capacity to learn: this wisdom about knowledge is the lesson.

Meaning in combination with hexahedron

With sufficient awareness of reality and of your own creative ability, you can achieve self-realization in the world during this lifetime. You allow yourself to experiment. You focus when necessary, and you make room for fun. Your leadership is about learning, maintaining boundaries and connecting, giving direction and co-creating.

The art of creation XIV

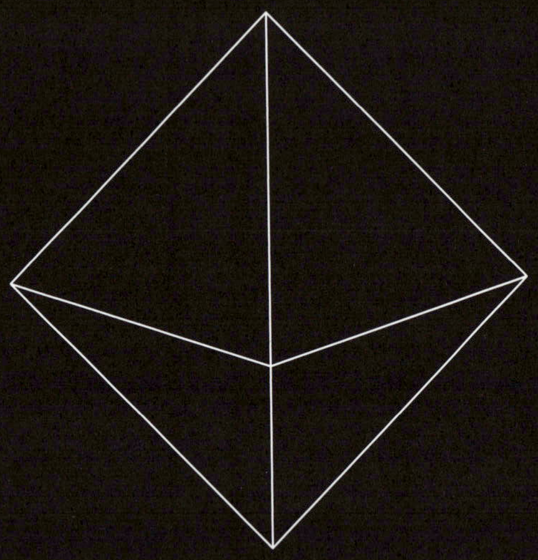

Octahedron series I – XIV

From knowledge to wisdom

In this card deck, the Octahedron series stands for the themes of 'astuteness', 'equality', 'balance' and 'clarity'. Difficult life situations involving sadness, loss, parting and struggle challenge you to achieve clarity and maturity. You learn to analyze situations better and become able to see yourself and others more clearly.

Essence

Experiencing a number of disappointing situations in a row can lead to a feeling of instability. Perhaps you're thinking about giving up, or you feel the urge to make drastic choices. We cannot control the outcomes of life processes. You can't think your way out of a problem. The intellectual argumentation of choices mainly costs energy. Don't believe everything you think. Come back to what it's really about: trusting in yourself. How can you be true to yourself in this?

Meaning in combination with octahedron

Be prepared to explain things. Communicate the essence, no more and no less. The situation requires you to be awake, to get to the core of the matter and to be authentic.

Awareness

Search for explicable facts. Spinning around trying to find an answer to 'why?' just keeps you stuck in thinking. Being aware that we 'don't know' brings acceptance. This gives us space to get to the active question 'how can I deal with this?' It removes you from of the feeling of powerlessness and puts you squarely back in your creative capacity.

Meaning in combination with octahedron

In order to become aware and eventually achieve realization, you first have to do something else. You need to sit in silence and honesty, and recognize your own part in the situation. Don't allow yourself to be drawn into self-condemnation, otherwise you'll miss the point. It's about being able to look at your own part neutrally, so you can achieve awareness. Once you can see your part, you can recognize the patterns in it and you won't have to repeat these experiences any longer.

Compassion

You can't simply decide to have compassion or empathy. However, you can learn to feel it. If someone shares their experience with you, try to connect to their world. Tune in to their perception. This shared experience will enable you to say: 'I understand what you mean.'

Meaning in combination with octahedron

You may think you're listening, but is that true? True listening is an experience, something that penetrates to a deeper layer. To actually listen is to hear with your heart. It starts with honoring where the other person is and accepting where you are now. This allows the dialog between you and the other to become a shared song, fed by heart energy. You can now be united in love.

Self-reflection

This is about looking at yourself and reflecting on yourself. It's illuminating your own process from different angles. The perspectives of others can give more nuance and more light. Consider what now helps you to take a step back so you can take a better look at yourself. Find out where your shadow parts play a role, where your ego may be playing tricks on you.

Meaning in combination with octahedron

It's about seeing yourself without filters or soft focus, about taking responsibility for yourself. If you can zoom out and get a clear view of the whole as well, you'll be able to understand why seeing yourself truly is so important: this expands everything.

Newborn time

This is the time for what's just been born. It's a kind of post-partum period for yourself or for a new project or relationship. Everything is still fresh and fragile. Perhaps the time leading up to this moment was difficult and stormy, or perhaps it took you a long time to get here. Either way, you need attention and silence in order to calibrate. Temperature, nutrition, rest, love; everything still has to come into balance. Masculine and feminine aspects are merging in the right measure and proportion.

Meaning in combination with octahedron

Before you can enter this newborn time, it's important to understand the lessons from the preceding time. Whatever you've experienced in the form of humiliation, loss or having to fight, it's important to process it properly so you can make a fresh, 'clean' start in this new period.

Shifting

Moments invite you to look and see how you can slide the 'crossfader' from one side to the other. Freedom is not about getting everything from the negative to the positive. Always living in the positive is an illusion and is also not freedom. Our experiences and our thinking sometimes tend more towards the positive and sometimes more towards the negative. True freedom lies in perceiving the shift. This awareness can help you to transcend all obstacles.

Meaning in combination with octahedron

This shift in perception requires an interlude. During this journey, you can find the nuances in shades of grey. What might seem dull or insignificant on the surface may bring perspective and movement.

Choices

There are no good or bad choices. Instead, there are tendencies to choose this or that. And there is doubt. This is because somewhere you believe that by making a particular choice right now, you could be doing something irrevocably and fatally right or wrong. Whether you choose quickly or hesitate for a long time, at a certain point you will make the choice. And then, one day, you'll find yourself living the answer in a natural way.

Meaning in combination with octahedron

Give up the tendency to gossip and manipulate. It's not necessary to get people on your side in order to make your own choices. All you have to do is share what you're dealing with. The conversation only really starts when you dare to fall silent while being together with others. This creates the space for you to be inspired to make new choices instead of manipulating the situation out of fear.

Life plan

Your life plan isn't just lying ready for you in a drawer in your head. It lives in your heart. Being able to express your higher purpose can involve a whole process. It requires authenticity and honesty. When looking into what your purpose is, you may find that what you thought you wanted so much turns out not to be true. You imposed it on yourself somewhere in the past, but now it's outdated, or perhaps it was never true at all. It can also be a lighter process; perhaps your life plan only needs a little updating as a result of new experiences and insights. Whatever the case may be, the process requires honesty and sometimes a serious investment in terms of attention and time.

Meaning in combination with octahedron

Postponing this investigation may seem safer than tackling it. Giving up habits, jeopardizing interests, feeling accountable; these things can frighten you into ignoring what's going on inside you. If you continue in this way, you'll end up stuck. Are you a slave to your ego, or is your consciousness in charge here?

Conversion

You can use your environment as a source of inspiration, but sometimes this doesn't work. Because you're in the compliance mode yourself, you accept the information in the outside world as being the systems or methods within which you should be working, and to which you have to adapt yourself. This doesn't feel good; you experience resistance and the inhibition of your creativity. Living freer from and freer in systems requires that you work in a different order. You can make this conversion yourself. Create from the inside out, instead of from the outside in. By doing this, you'll be able to freely use everything that's offered to you from the outside for your own growth. And you'll be able to bring out everything that you've developed within, to share its added value with others.

Meaning in combination with octahedron

Whenever you notice that you're becoming reactive, turn inwards first and then outwards again. When you become proficient in moving this way, you'll be able to transcend your reactivity and enter creativity. Possessing this skill will make you a huge source of inspiration for others. You'll be able to show others the way – first turn inwards, then outwards – by consistently doing this yourself. The only way out, is in :)

Communication

Your communication is often in relationship to the outside world. Perhaps you feel a great need to talk to others, and you have a tendency to say a lot.
But if you skip the inner conversation with yourself, this can lead to miscommunication with others.
How do you communicate with yourself? Do you listen to your body? Can you distinguish your thoughts from your mind? What kind of connection do you have between your physical and mental self? And are you able to experience that you perceive all your thoughts, feelings and sensations, but that you are not them?

Meaning in combination with octahedron

This is about recognizing what you're pushing away, but also seeing how you're stifling yourself. This will continue until something from outside stops it.
Do you want to wait for that? How long will you stay shut off? What's real doesn't have to be thought up first, or wait for the right moment. The point is that you tell it from the heart.

Acceptance

The pursuit of ideals may stem from a lack of self-acceptance. This makes the desire to 'improve the world' a projection of the idea that you have to improve yourself. Conversely, when idealism stems from self-acceptance and self-love, the energy is often softer; rather than being against something, it's for something. It's less fanatic and more natural. I can do this or give it for free, because my heart is overflowing with it. You can examine this impulse by checking to see whether you're looking for attention, recognition and compliments, or whether it makes little difference to you and you're just doing it because you want to.

Meaning in combination with octahedron

Acceptance of who you are and of the situation prevents you from becoming overconfident. You have something good to share. It's not necessary to become fanatic, persuasive or malicious about it. Honor where the other is, accept the world, know where you come from. Acceptance is the basis for all change.

Purity

Being yourself, being authentic, is not something you can resolve to do: it's a process. Once you've broken through certain patterns, you may feel more real, but also naked and vulnerable at first. Without your familiar stories, you suddenly find yourself standing there, feeling a little embarrassed, in your undershirt. There's no new way of being yet, and perhaps there won't be one either. You have to get used to acting and reacting in the present, without drama, methods or strategy. There is no immediate applause for your efforts. But being true to yourself slowly but surely gives you something else that you can get used to: the feeling that you're alive, and that any moment can be authentic, fresh and new.

Meaning in combination with octahedron

It's a terrible shame to try and shut off your sensitivity out of fear of your own purity. It is precisely this sensitivity, this blushing authenticity, that makes it possible for you to be innovative. From this position, you can also be a good facilitator in group processes, bringing purity into cultures. This refreshing capacity can bring about a lot of change in a very light way.

Talent

You can transcend the idea of 'my talent' to realize that you've been given a gift for this life. When the ego no longer claims this, you may experience a feeling of gratitude washing over you. There may also be feelings of grief. What you first stood for no longer seems so important. Yet it is. You can enrich your environment with something that feels completely normal to you. Your specific gift is your autonomous form of giving love. The ego is the only one to miss the compliments.

Meaning in combination with octahedron

What you're good at becomes subtler, less obtrusive. Less visible but more permeable. You can exert all your influence by emanating and exhaling. When you let go of the need to be 'cool', you can become the cooling factor when things get heated. Your contribution leads to relaxation, which is another word for trust. Do you understand how valuable this is? This gift allows you to truly share and receive. This makes 'talent' the stuff of pure magic.

Confirmation

When you're no longer focused on gaining recognition from others, you can be more open to subtler forms of confirmation. You can broadcast your thoughts or ideas a little more and see them reflected in reality. This gives confidence, peace and a lot of inner enjoyment too.

Meaning in combination with octahedron

Sometimes you're amazed by how clearly you can express things, how heightened your thinking is, how effortlessly things go. You no longer feel the need to reap the rewards or brag about your own achievements. This doesn't mean that you should disregard yourself, it's more about 'relaxing into your autonomy'. You can now lean back and enjoy everything that comes your way naturally.

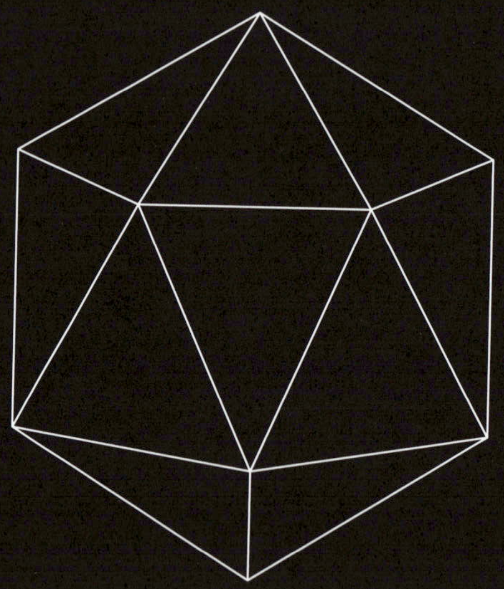

Icosahedron series I – XIV

Unconditional love

In this card deck, the Icosahedron series stands for the themes of 'relationships', 'family', 'passion' and 'sexuality'. Your connection with the other and associated experiences of loneliness, rejection, merging and pure love are offered to you so you can learn to love without conditions. To merge while remaining true to yourself: that's the most fruitful dynamic in love and relationships.

Security

We often seek that feeling of 'home' in others: relationships, family, friends. Having a home base gives you a safe, secure feeling. This can become so important to you that you hold on to it anxiously, even if this 'home' isn't actually cozy or safe at all. Your true home, the place of true safety to which you can always go, is closer than you think. Home is within, where your heart lives.

Meaning in combination with icosahedron

If you feel at home with yourself, you won't need to look for security among others. Experiencing the emptiness and starting to fulfill yourself begins with exploring the questions 'what do I need?' and 'how can I take care of myself?'

Unconditionality

It's only when the conviction that you need to improve yourself disappears that you'll be able to love unconditionally. After the realization 'I don't have to be different than I am' comes a deep calmness. With this realization, you'll notice that the other also no longer has to be different. You love that other person unconditionally: not for what he or she does or doesn't do, but for who he or she is. Indeed, simply because he or she exists and is there. Love is a state in which you can exist unconditionally, both individually and together.

Meaning in combination with icosahedron

Love can take on a new meaning and your relationship enter a liberating phase. True connection means that a relationship is no longer something to be maintained, or a recurring topic of conversation. Your experience of sexuality can also change when you have no expectations of how it should be.

Unconditional love II

Satisfaction

Creating a life that doesn't actually suit you, or maintaining relationships in which you no longer feel at home, will not fulfill you. When you act out of a need for recognition or affirmation, the results will never be satisfactory and the compliments will never be enough. Which projects and relationships bring you pleasure, and fascinate and inspire you? Invest in these processes and allow them to grow by cultivating them.

Meaning in combination with icosahedron

Once conditional love transcends to become unconditional love and you often find yourself in a state of love, you may experience an intense sense of gratitude. At first you may have thought that gratitude was a form of politeness, something that you 'had to' be, but now you can experience its true depth. Together, gratitude and unconditional love are a recipe for bliss; a peaceful kind of ecstasy that you can ignite in others.

Unconditional love III

Disconnecting

Confusing thoughts and feelings. Words, stories, experiences, your own emotions and the emotions of others; these all get stuck in your system. If these disruptions influence your behavior, that can affect your relationships. Perhaps you have a tendency to be defensive, or you're easily irritated. Withdrawing for a moment from the commotion prevents you from being overwhelmed by external impulses. If you've made too many connections, you can protect yourself a little more by disconnecting yourself momentarily from the outside world.

Meaning in combination with icosahedron

Forcing yourself to be among people now or attend occasions because you think you have to can make you feel anxious or cut off. You'd be better off examining why you feel this social duty. What do you have to lose? What is the underlying conviction, which may not be true at all, but which you believe anyway? Maintaining something that is so disruptive is neither loving to yourself nor to others.

Forgiveness

When you live from your heart, there is no such thing as the wrong action. Even if it seems you've done something 'wrong', that's no reason to judge yourself. It's a moment for self-examination and forgiveness. Looking at your actions without judgment will allow room for understanding and growth. Only that will make you wiser.

Meaning in combination with icosahedron

If you look more deeply at your own guilt, you'll see that, strangely enough, you may also be addicted to the feeling. Seeking to understand your own mechanisms will also make you feel the pain you've been trying to avoid for so long. It's not fun, but it'll bring about one of the most beautiful things you can give yourself in this life: forgiveness.

Revelation

It's time to reveal yourself. When the world overwhelms you, you may react by retreating further and further into yourself, until you're completely locked away. Everything outside feels unsafe and hostile. The inner world no longer brings liberation; it has become a self-built prison. The exercise now is to go the other way: not to turn inwards, but to bring yourself outwards. You can start small. In the end, you'll show what you're keeping concealed inside. This coming out is about being your own beautiful self in the world. Shine on, you crazy diamond.

Meaning in combination with icosahedron

The moment you go onto the stage, you may immediately want to vanish backstage again. But you've already been seen. Take your up your position on stage, and surrender. Share, flow, speak. Seize your moment.

Patience

You can't get rid of impatience by exerting pressure or control. What is the source of your restlessness? Often, impatience is a sign that you've created a particular image or expectation as to the way something should happen, and how fast. This is driven by survival thoughts such as: 'Otherwise I might be too late.' These thoughts are practical in survival situations, or if you have to catch a train, but they have a limiting effect when it comes to bringing something to life.

Meaning in combination with icosahedron

When you give something attention, it comes to life. And the more you look, the more you see. If you view your life through a crystal ball, you'll see it's full of miracles. This will be a dream time if you dare to let it happen!

Desire

This is about being able to distinguish between your needs and your desires. Beneath an immediate need, a deeper desire may be hidden that is blocked by a conviction. For example, the desire for recognition may express a need that reflects a deeper desire for self-acceptance, which is blocked by a false sense of not being good enough.

Meaning in combination with icosahedron

Nothing that you experience is personal. Whatever others do to you is a projection or expression of what they apparently have to live out and learn or not learn. Actually, it's not about you at all. You can choose to either give in to melancholy or seek out the love and the deeper desire within yourself.

Inner freedom

You don't feel free to do or say what you want. You may experience opposition in various situations, which means that everything costs energy. The things you normally enjoy are difficult, as if you can't do anything right. We can't blame others for our inner struggle. Give yourself permission to express yourself in a loving but clear way. What do you want? What don't you want? Be clear, and don't be needy.

Meaning in combination with icosahedron

Once you begin to feel free in yourself, you may experience this as a feeling of being pregnant with something, or that something is in the air. At first it feels like a quiet happiness inside, followed by the feeling that you can finally allow yourself to celebrate life. The mood of this party is somewhere between being madly in love and celebrating your birthday.

Sexuality

Sexuality is one of the most powerful energies you can experience as a human being, both together and alone. Sexual energy acts as a catalyst; it is a driving creative energy. It's a very personal paradigm of fire, excitement, desire, ecstasy, release and creation. Sexuality takes place in the here and now. It's true, naked surrender to being and togetherness.

Meaning in combination with icosahedron

It's a feeling of coming home, in your own body and/or together with each other. This encounter is a fertilization that can lead to intimacy, creativity, flow and bliss.

Contact

Searching for the truth, for the real. It sometimes feels impossible to get there. Or you're projecting it onto your connection with others or things outside yourself. First find the connection within: out of your head, through your heart. What are you observing? What are you experiencing? By first going within, you can connect at the most subtle level and feel the life in everything. Within, here, now: this is contact.

Meaning in combination with the icosahedron

You can make gentler contact with the other based on the connection you have with yourself, in a way that's not so needy & greedy. You're more nuanced, more careful. From your shared interest you can see where energy should be invested. You are simultaneously softer and tougher when dealing with the other. There to be loved.

Unconditional love XI

Self-esteem

Learn to appreciate yourself. Not on the level of the ego; self-esteem goes deeper than that. It's about seeing where your autonomy lies. The prerequisite for this clear vision is recognizing your right to exist. You are allowed to exist simply because you do exist, period. This realization is the starting point from which you can look at your being, your person, your talents and your opportunities without any claim or judgment. Learning to appreciate yourself in order to get the best out of yourself is the reason you're here.

Meaning in combination with icosahedron

When you realize your own value, you'll be better at appreciating others for who they are. Relationships that arise from self-esteem and appreciation for the other ensure that the differences add value to the connection. Your 'being different' does not compete, it is complementary.

Intuition

The fresh, unbiased observation in the present moment, is the pure feeling known as intuition. It goes beyond thinking and beyond emotion. It's not an insight that simply drops into your mind. It's a subtle trait, a form of perceiving or receiving. Most of the time, our thoughts and feelings get in the way of it. Some confuse intuition with beliefs and emotions. Intuition is about the process of going within and observing what's happening at the energetic level. Intuition wants nothing and has no opinion. It's quiet, because it's an inner knowing.

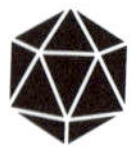

Meaning in combination with icosahedron

You're connected to your higher self and yet remain firmly grounded. This enables you to be an expert on your own feelings. If you've lost this connection, it's a good idea to seek help from someone who (at this moment, at least) is strongly 'vertically' aligned.

Unconditional love XIII

Blueprint

We all have our own programming that comes through our experiences and characteristics: our preferences, fears, desires, blind spots, and so on. It makes us who we've become, and sometimes it also makes us stuck, either in how we react to others or judge ourselves. What was once fluid solidifies; our ideas become dogmas. What used to be an expansive vision now seems to be a rigid system. However, your true nature is not a fixed pattern but a living work of art, based on the deeper desire to be free.

Meaning in combination with the icosahedron

In order to develop leadership, it can sometimes be a good idea to enter into an apprenticeship with someone for a time, all the while knowing that he or she does not have a monopoly on the whole truth. Once you acknowledge that you'll always be a student, you can be a true master.

Unconditional love XIV

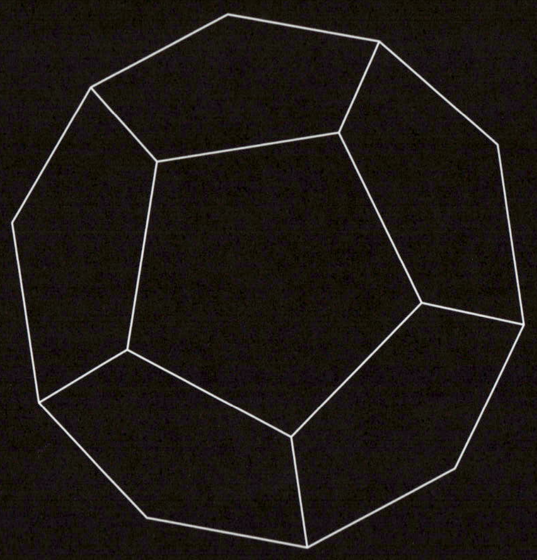

Dodecahedron series I – XIV

From ego to authenticity

In this card deck, the Dodecahedron series stands for themes such as 'self-expression', 'assertiveness' and 'autonomy'. Life challenges you to show yourself, to express yourself in your own way, to stand up for yourself, and to use your voice. This is about fully taking your place in this world from the position of a natural right to exist that is free from ego; being allowed to exist because you exist.

Authenticity

A change process resulting in authenticity requires you to release the prevailing opinions in your culture and in your own thinking. Focus more on who you are, rather than comparing yourself with others. Declaring your own colors and bringing them into sharper focus helps you to better resist both the feeling that you have to comply and the tendency to imitate others or adopt opinions without question.

Meaning in combination with dodecahedron

You grow up in an environment where certain habits, tastes and opinions prevail. Within your circle of friends or in your relationship too, you agree on many things. But within your own culture, you may also notice how you differ from others. In this, you can discover your individuality. Which of your preferences and characteristics are not so much culturally determined, but are really your own?

Expansion

You can see your energy field as similar to breathing: it can expand and contract. You can take in energy and send it out. Just as with breathing, you can learn to experience and regulate this energy field more consciously, shrinking or enlarge the field around you. Visualizing can help with this, while using your breathing as support.

Meaning in combination with dodecahedron

Developing decisiveness and focus can be seen as breathing. You go within to process things and gather courage, and you turn outwards to take the next step. Focusing works the same way: zooming out in order to be able to zoom in again. Seeing your capacity for expansion as an inward and outward movement enables you to occupy your space more consciously.

Rhythm

You're often so identified with what you're doing that you think you're the doer. All the time, however, there's an observer watching that active figure. If you take the observer's position, you can better see how you move and which rhythms you follow. Are you in gear, are you synchronized with your circumstances, or are you out of step with what's going on? Looking at your life phases and your own movements provides information that helps you to find the right rhythm.

Meaning in combination with dodecahedron

You may need to repeat moves to a certain degree in order to discover a pattern. Karma is a dance which keeps repeating itself until you're able to distinguish your movements correctly. If you can determine how a particular attitude comes about, you'll be able to get to the next, new movement.

Pride

Pride may seem like an ego thing. However, there is an enlightened version, just as false modesty is the shadow version of modesty. What is the pure form of pride, and how is it useful? If you don't invest your pride in the ego by inflating yourself with it or by replacing it with false modesty, then pride can be a form of acknowledging yourself. You take a moment to consider having reached a certain point in your development, and you're satisfied about getting there. Seeing what you're capable of without judgment affirms and empowers you.

Meaning in combination with dodecahedron

Somehow you're happy that you've got here, but you also feel that you're not quite fully here yet. Perhaps you're noticing a feeling of tension that you need to deal with. Sometimes it's good to set aside your pride and engage in an open confrontation. Pride can stand in the way of growth.

Vulnerability

When you want to connect with other people, showing your vulnerability (that you can be touched or affected) is a very good 'strategy'. The other can feel that you've laid down your shield or weapons. From a position of calmness, you can connect with someone at a deeper level. This allows growth and development in you and in your relationships. Only the ego can be hurt; the soul cannot. All the pain and little wounds you might experience by being vulnerable are exercises in moving from ego to being authentic.

Meaning in combination with dodecahedron

You may have to get accustomed to the idea of being touched or affected in relation to other people. Uncertainty makes you fall back into old patterns of closing off, defensiveness or retreating into convictions. It helps to replace 'I think' with 'I notice'; for example, you could say 'I notice I'm feeling some resistance' instead of 'I think this is bad.' That is, make an observation instead of stating your opinion.

Awakening

You have the feeling that nothing's working any more; you've tried everything. All of your options seem to have withered away. When you're moving cyclically, everything you've believed in is peeled away, layer by layer: this path is a dead end, this idea has come to nothing, that's an illusion... 'Is this it then? Am I nothing at all?' If you ultimately turn out to be essentially nothing or no one, you'll wake up, free of the idea that you're supposed to be anything in particular. You no longer have to be somebody: 'I am' simply becomes 'being'.

Meaning in combination with dodecahedron

This is about staying in 'being' and always returning to this state. The starting point for your actions has changed. You're less concerned within yourself about what you're doing externally. There's less stress, less strategy, less guilt. You're mainly engaged in observing rather than having opinions. This is what it's like to be awake: to be there without judgment, free from excessive planning, the need to draw conclusions, having expectations, forming opinions.

Self-healing

The constant need for something outside yourself to numb your pain or discomfort can lead to much agitation. You might briefly find a source of relief, a fix, a band-aid or a kick, and then the next pain comes along. You create your own suffering by longing to 'feel good', to be rid of something, to move onto the next moment already. Learning to simply be with anxiety or pain is the key to your self-healing capacity. Don't panic, don't suppress the pain, just experience it, until you experience that it changes on its own. Now you have the proof that you're the observer; you are not your pain.

Meaning in combination with dodecahedron

Experience your emotions and sensations as movements in your body and energy system. Self-healing is a question of time and paying attention to stimuli and signs. It's not about having an opinion about what you're feeling, but about letting it go, like a mother who holds her weeping child until he or she has finished crying. Rather than saying 'hush now', saying 'it's all right' instead. Self-healing is the deepest form of care and comfort. This exercise sometimes brings great insights, as if you're cracking a code.

Decisiveness

Endless circling in both thoughts and speech gets boring. Once you tire of your own fuss, you'll begin to recognize your patterns. Each time you catch yourself repeating your stories as a way of preventing yourself moving forward, take a break. There's no point in judging yourself, however; it's about the realization of 'hey, I'm doing it again'. This is the alarm signal that will eventually lead you to be decisive and take action.

Meaning in combination with dodecahedron

Every time you feel fear come up in you, just smile and allow it to be there. Decisiveness does not necessarily mean that you have to be very strong. It's about working smartly with your strengths. Breathe in your fear in order to release power on exhalation. Kung Fu power.

Creation

Creation is not a mental process; instead, it's the realm of the imagination. Everything you manifest starts with an idea. However, we more often use our capacity to visualize and then to realize in a negative rather than positive sense. For example, right before we fall asleep we spend time worrying about things. While that's actually a perfect time to do something you probably did much more often as a child: fantasize! The imagination game is a wonderful driver for realization.

Meaning in combination with dodecahedron

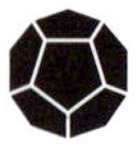

You can free up the ways of learning that you'd left behind in your childhood and bring them to life once more. Fun, play and discovery are serious tactics that you can consciously use to achieve creativity and productivity.

Synchronicity

Synchronicity is the recognition of symbols in everyday life. You may sometimes find yourself in a period in which you experience many coincidences. You can see this as a sign that you're 'on track', and that your life is aligned with your deeper desires. Not only can you view these coincidences as encouragement, you can also try to 'read' them more deeply. 'What could this be telling me, and what can I do with it?' You develop a keener way of viewing things that allows you to use coincidences as a kind of life coach.

Meaning in combination with dodecahedron

Experiencing synchronicity can have an affirming or deepening effect. You may also find yourself unable to understand the precise 'intention' of it, and you're left instead with a feeling of wonder, surprise or excitement. If you're open to it, ordinary life can be magical.

Birth

Sometimes when you're going through a process, you need a clean slate in order to move forward. You're no longer thinking the way you did or doing what you did, but starting completely afresh. 'Kill your darling' sometimes feels as if you're losing something, but it can be very liberating. Think of that one sentence that's stopping you from being fresh and free. Pull those words out of your thoughts, crumple them up and throw them in the bin, and start over.

Meaning in combination with dodecahedron

It may be that there's still something you have to complete before being able to start afresh. You may not feel like dealing with it, but it keeps gnawing at you. Ask yourself whether you still have something you need to say or talk about. Or is it something that you have to process within yourself? Tackling it now will mean you won't have to deal with it later.

From ego to authenticity XI

Turning point

Not all days are equally inspiring. It can be this way for a little while, but sometimes it really goes on for too long. Then you'll experience a feeling of resistance, and waiting for something to change will no longer be an option. What you first experienced as a minor irritation is now seriously uncomfortable. Apply the brakes and change direction.

Meaning in combination with dodecahedron

Saying 'yes' to life sometimes starts with saying 'no'. Perhaps you have the tendency to react to something and then later feel uncomfortable about what you've said or done. You can go back and review the situation. It's a good exercise in setting your boundaries.

Clarity

You may sometimes feel you're not being clear enough about your wishes or your boundaries, with respect to others or yourself. Perhaps there are too many choices, or you still need to think things through, or it's scary to be clear because you're afraid of committing yourself or afraid of the reactions of others. Try to get clear on what the essence is of your boundary or wish, then state what you do and don't want. It's not necessary to try and convince yourself, or to doubt yourself again. Share your wish or boundary, see what happens, repeat your message if necessary, and wait quietly.

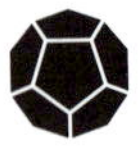

Meaning in combination with dodecahedron

Sometimes you have an extremely strong urge to say something, and now! When this happens, you can turn your attention inwards and look to see where the feeling of 'emergence' (something is coming up) switches over into 'emergency' (this has to happen now!). Communicating what's important to you from a place of calmness is often a much more powerful act.

Synergy

The whole is greater than the sum of its parts. It's about a collaboration that delivers more than the individual parts combined. Good synergy can arise between people, but also in your own development process. Whenever the heart is your guide and the ego is at its service, there's space to create something that joins everything into a greater whole. Clear expectations and clear communication can help a great deal in creating synergy.

Meaning in combination with dodecahedron

When the exchange can take place between people without unclear expectations, trust can grow.
If we don't see differences as rejections, but instead accept each other's individuality, it becomes clear where you meet and where you can diverge. Synergy isn't something you can agree upon, it's something that arises. The intention to be authentic and honest, to show yourself, is what makes this possible.

Spreads

Shuffle the cards carefully before laying out a spread. Then fan them out in a semicircle in front of you and hover the palm of your left hand over them to feel which cards speak to you. Choose these cards for your spread.

Spread 1 - Life question

Card 1

1. What is the meaning of this event?

Spread 2 - The learning process

Card 1	Card 2	Card 3
1. now	2. past	3. future

Spread 3 - Family work

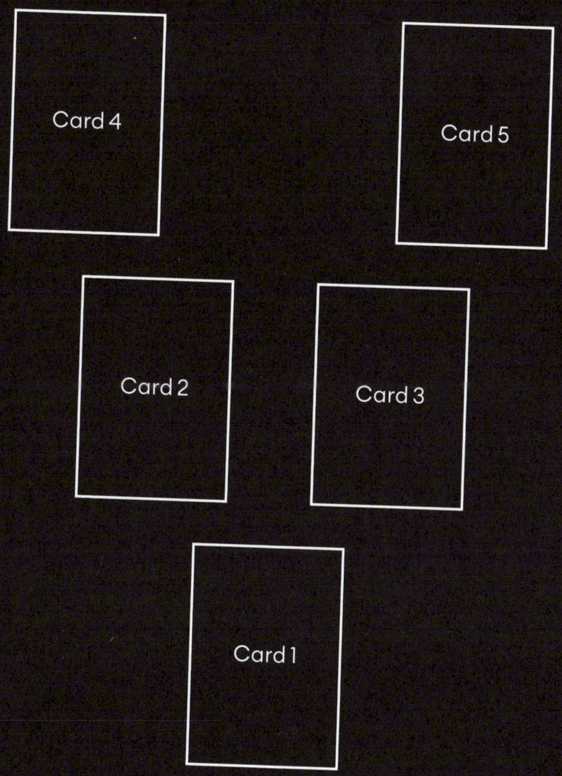

1. your soul task in this life
2. mother's task
3. father's task
4. work of mother's ancestors
5. work of father's ancestors

Spread 4 - Soul purpose

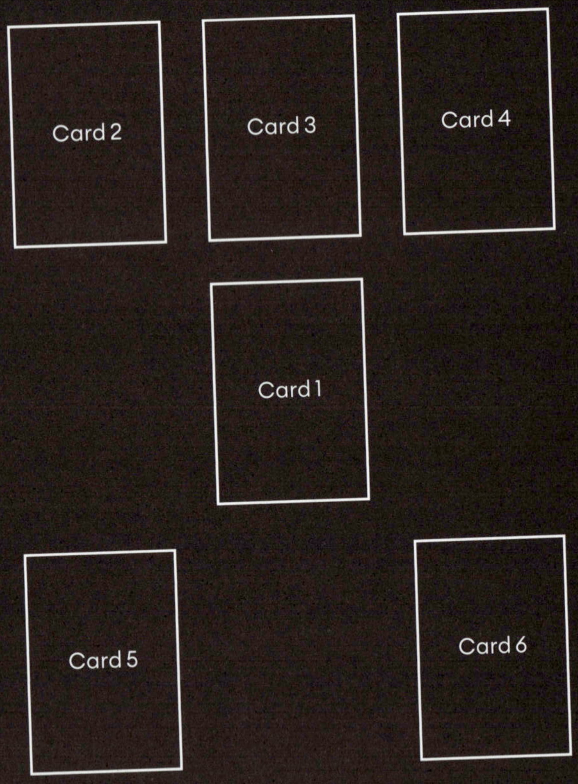

1. you now
2. past destination
3. present destination
4. future destination
5. obstacle
6. liberation

Spread 5 - Love relationships

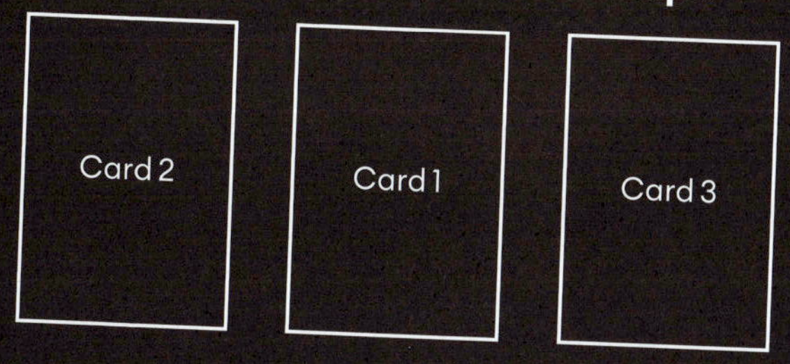

1. self-love
2. relational love
3. unconditional love

Spread 6 - Your energy system

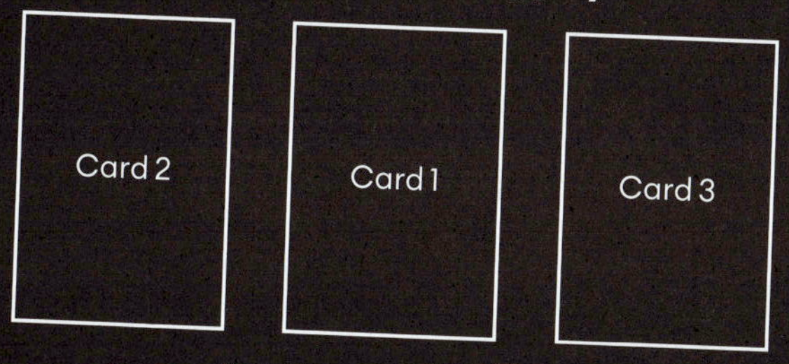

1. your energy level now
2. what you are sensitive to
3. what you could radiate more

Colophon

inner.space - Sacred Geometry Tarot deck & guide

Concept: inner.space
Core content and geometric patterns: Janosh
Design: Dietwee –brand, design and communication, dietwee.nl
Text + final editing: Gitta de Leeuw + Albert Wiglema, fromhere.eu
Translation: languagelab.nl
Printed in China: chingluen.com

ISBN: 978 90 9031 692 5
NUR: 720

www.inner.space

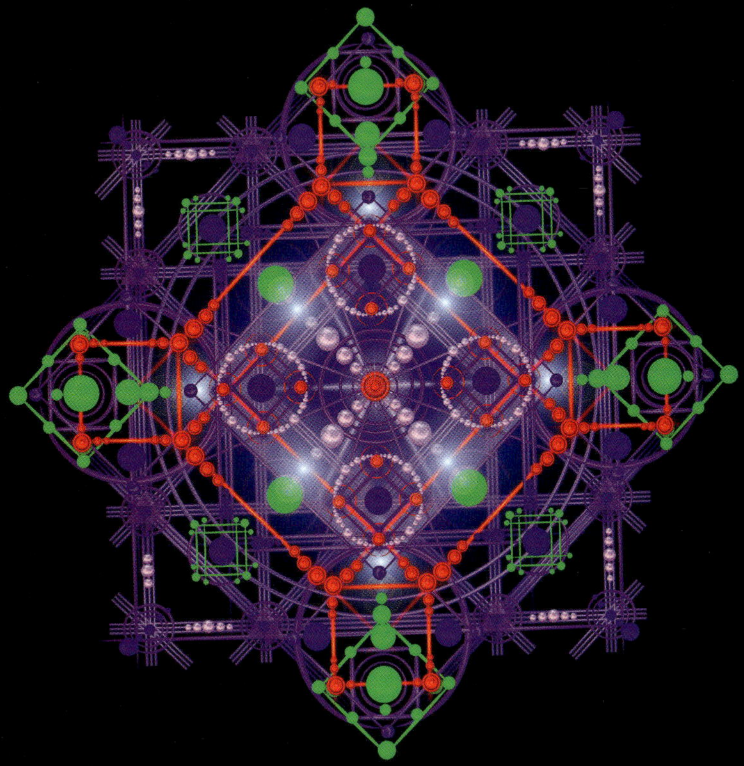

The life cycle I

Harmony

inner space

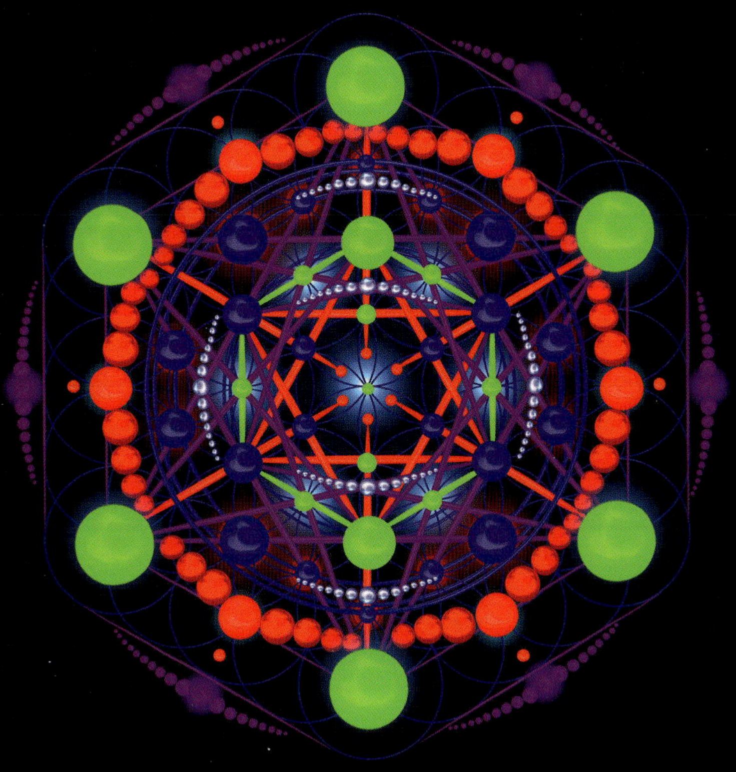

The life cycle II

Limitlessness

inner space

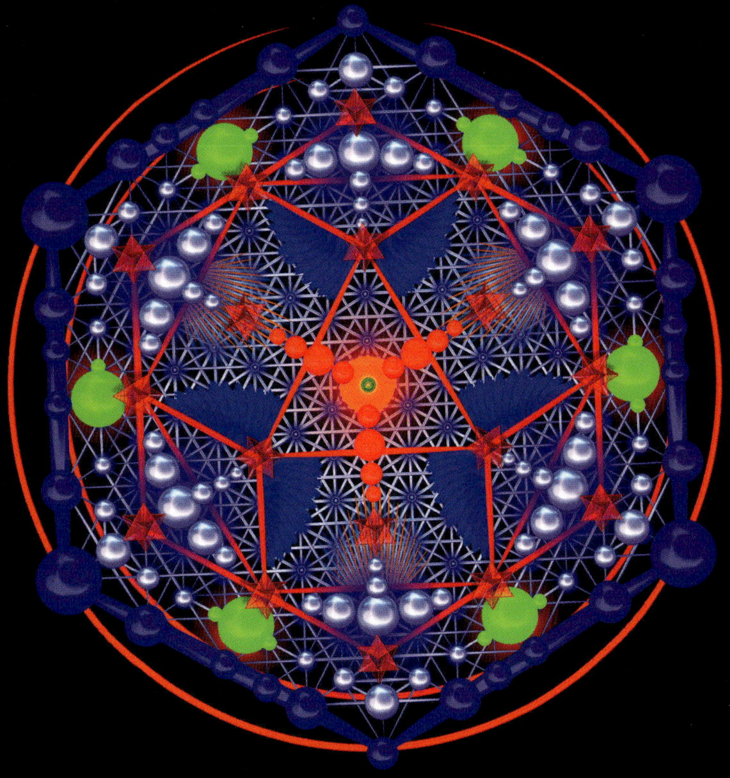

The life cycle III

Inner voice

inner space

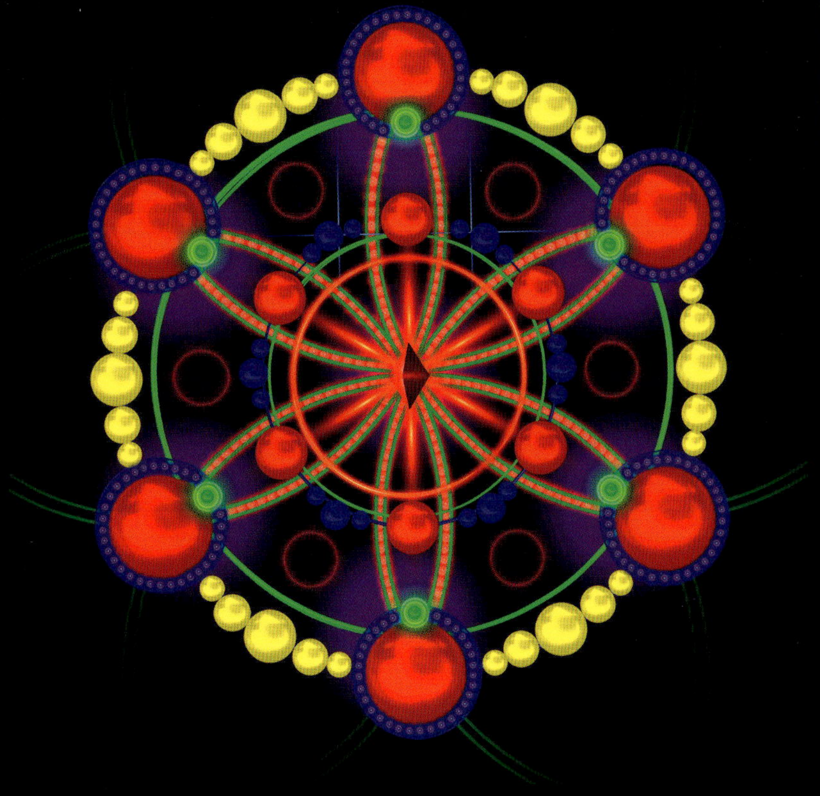

The life cycle IV
Initiation

inner space

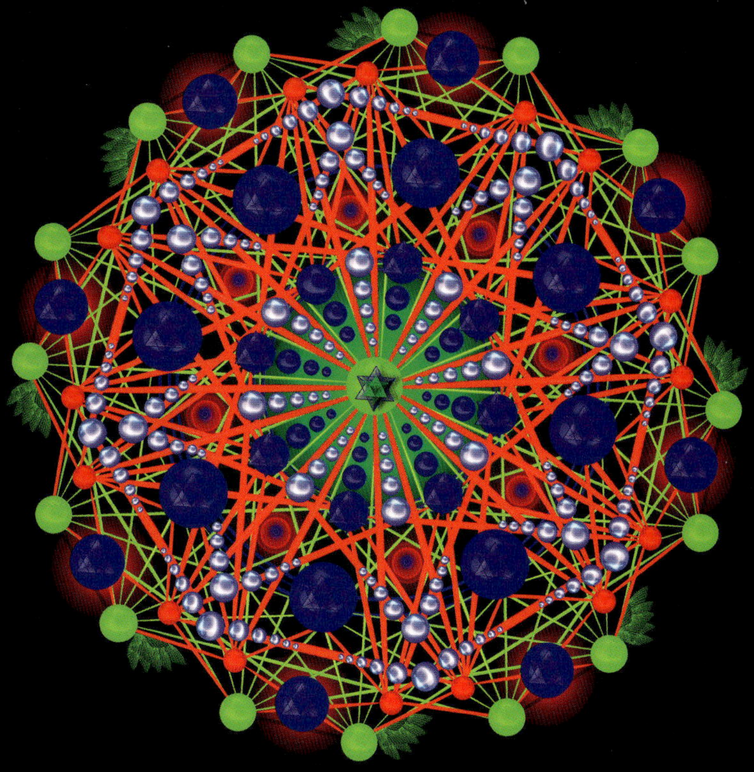

The life cycle V
Christ consciousness

inner space

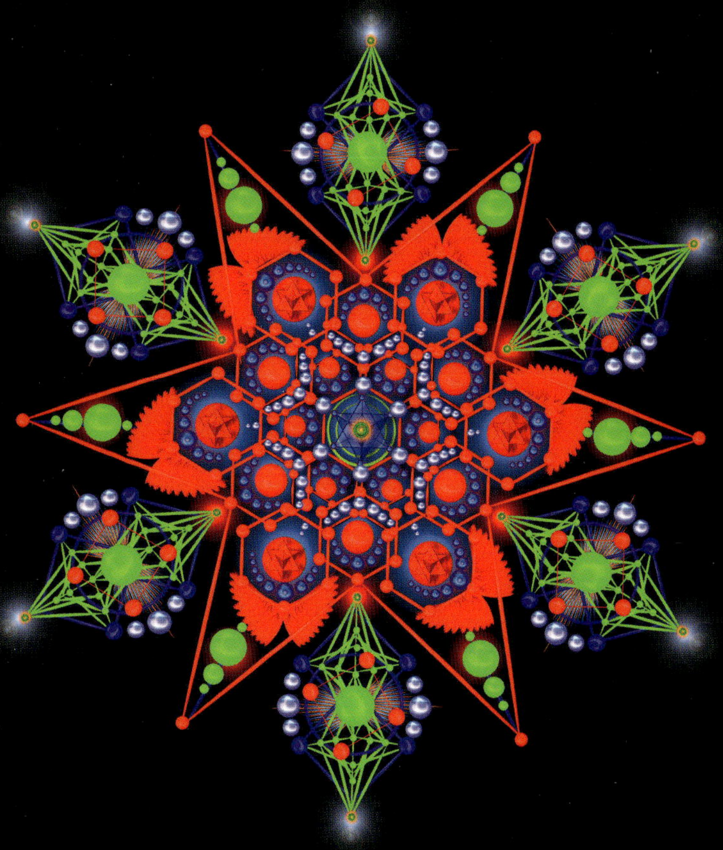

The life cycle VI

Mastery

inner space

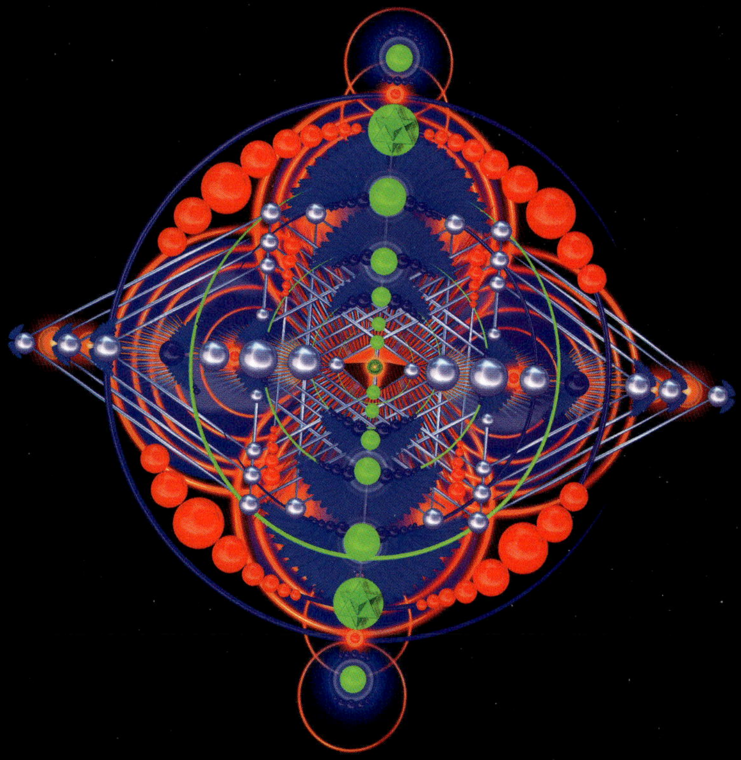

The life cycle VII
Reunification

inner space

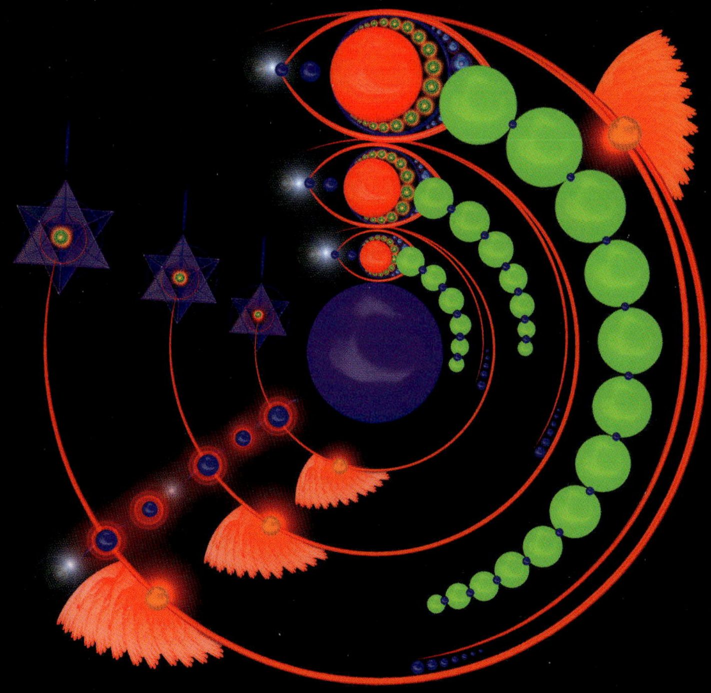

The life cycle VIII

Transcendence

inner space

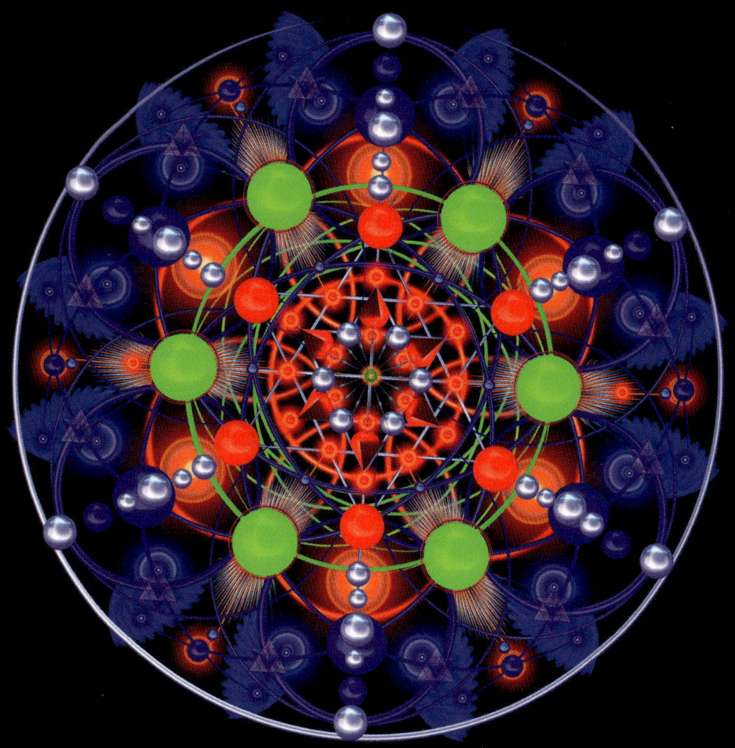

The life cycle IX
Self-love

inner space

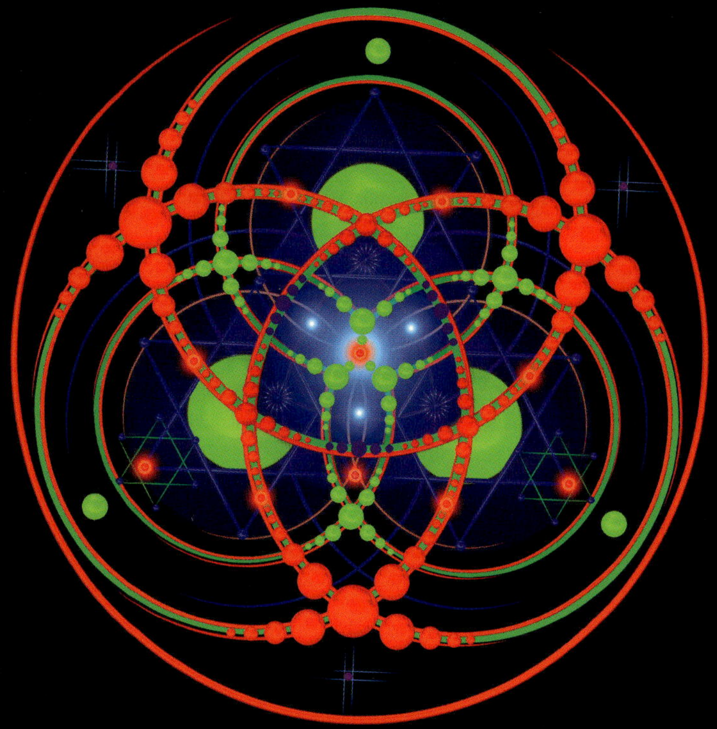

The life cycle X

Commitment

inner space

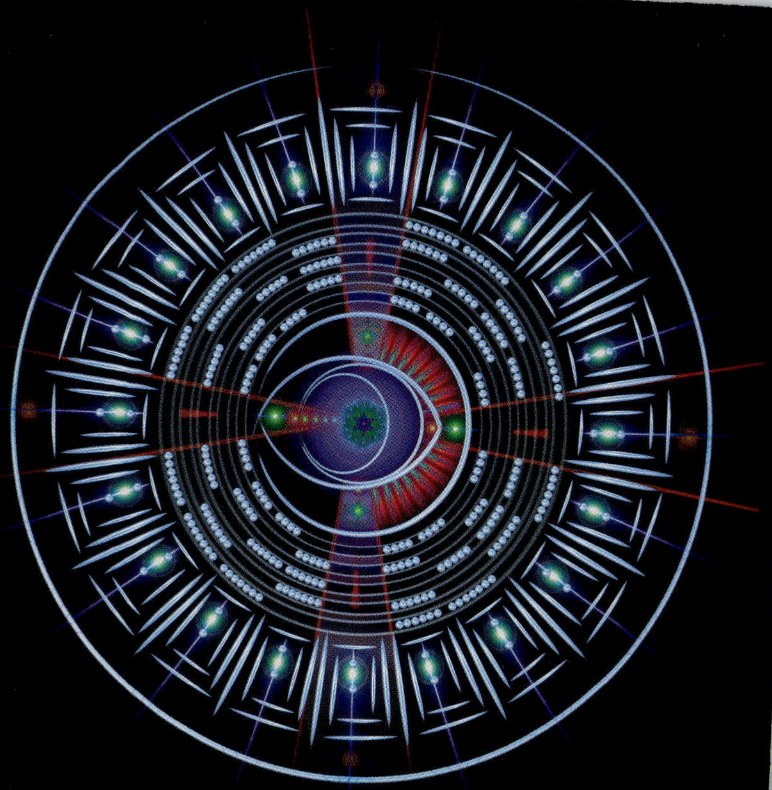

The life cycle XI
Abundance

inner space

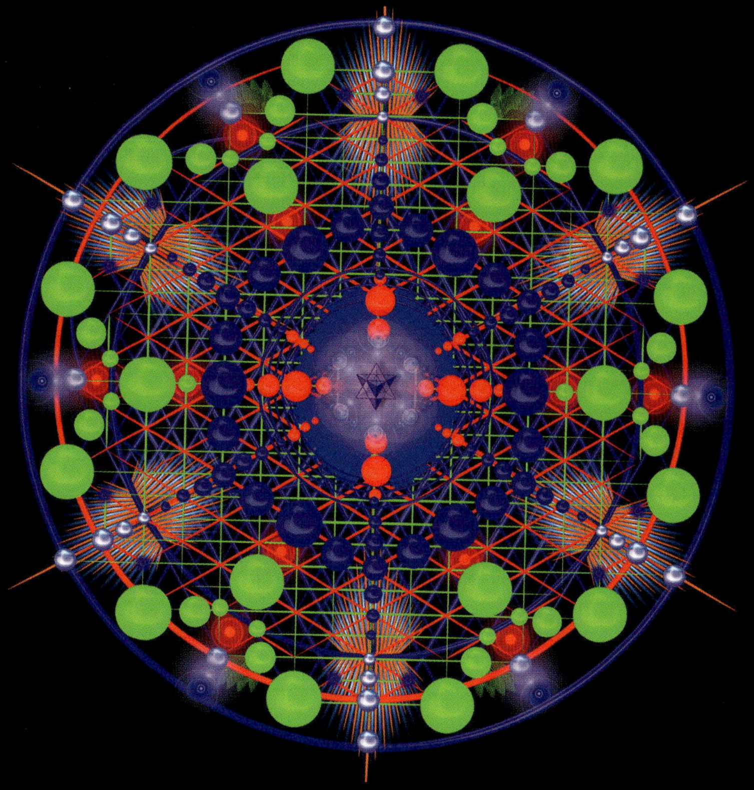

The life cycle XII
Resonance

inner space

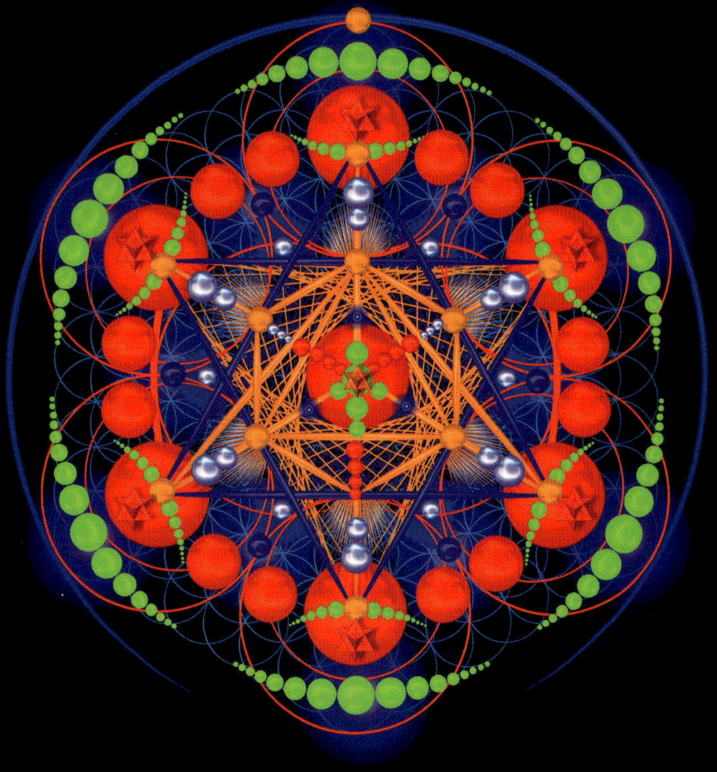

The life cycle XIII

Reconsideration

inner space

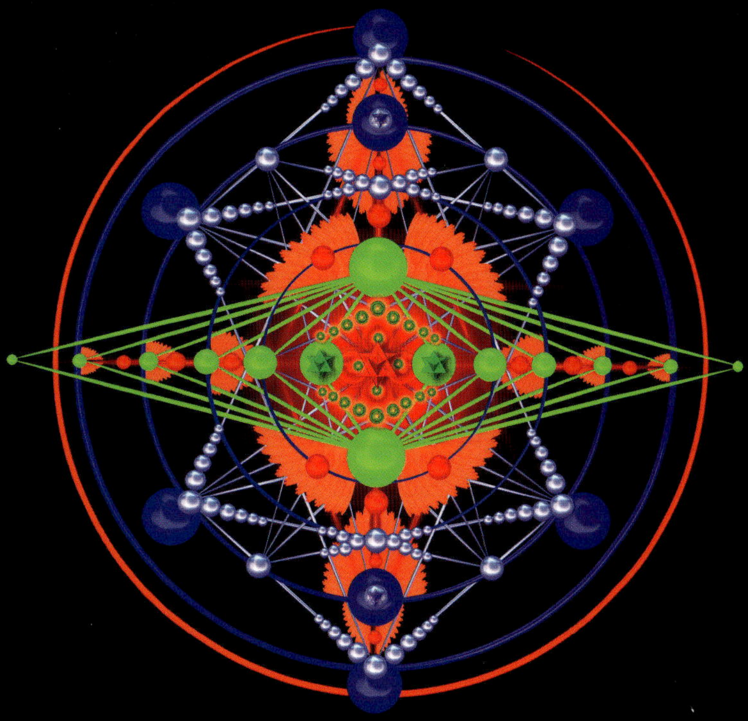

The life cycle XIV
Unfolding

inner space

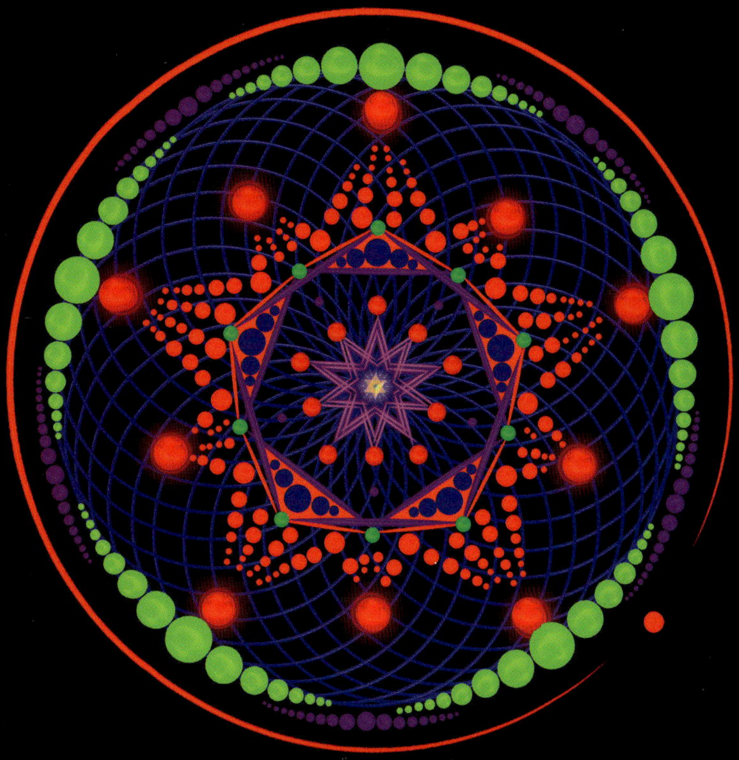

The life cycle XV
Ascension

inner space

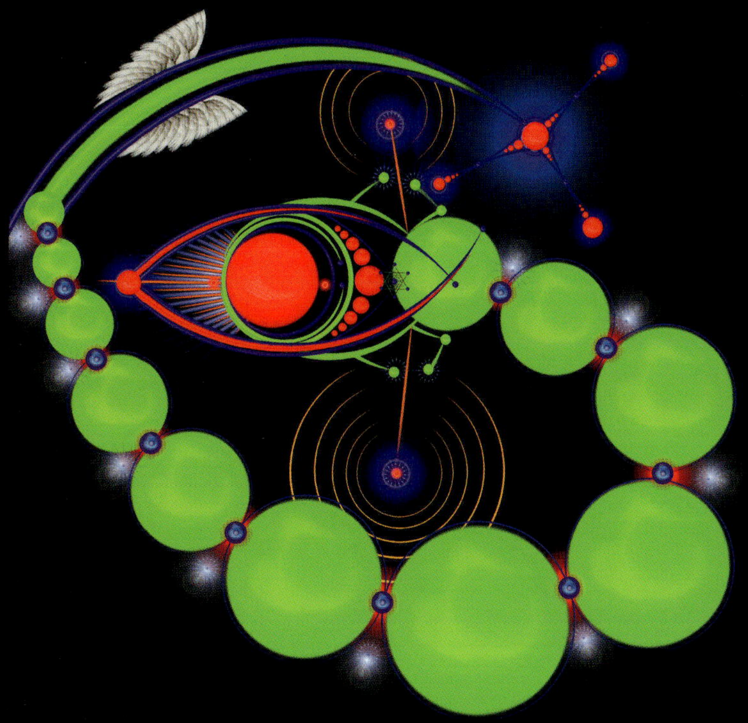

The life cycle XVI
Unmasking

inner space

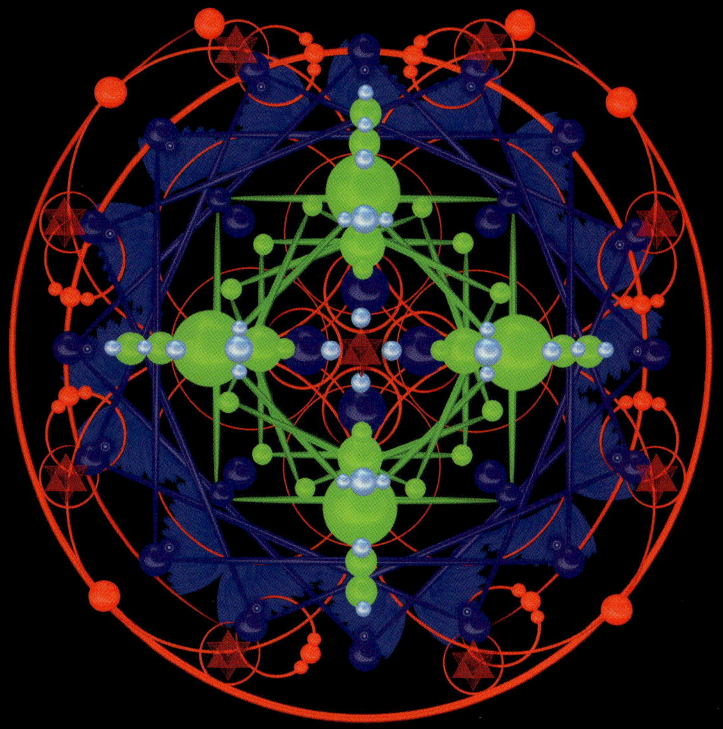

The life cycle XVII
Reforming

inner space

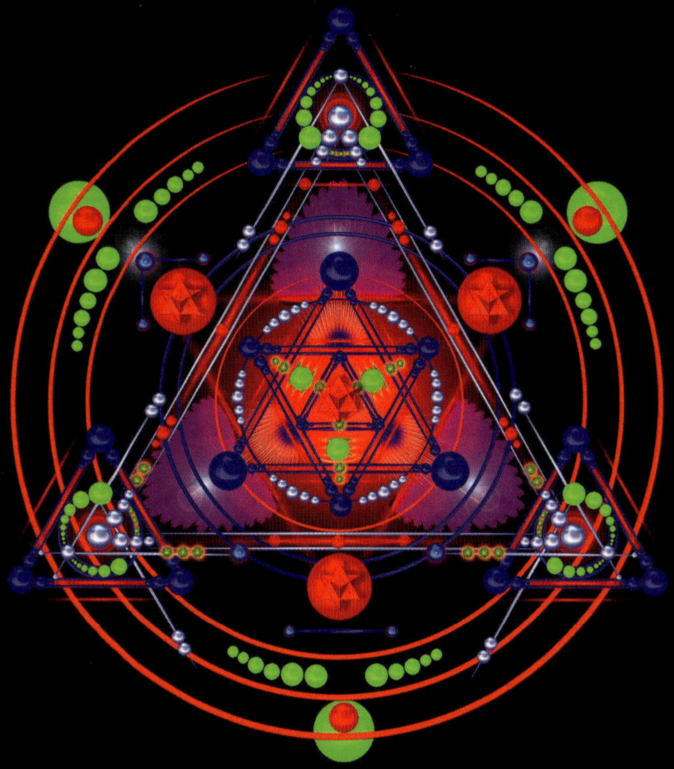

The life cycle XVIII
Osmosis

inner space

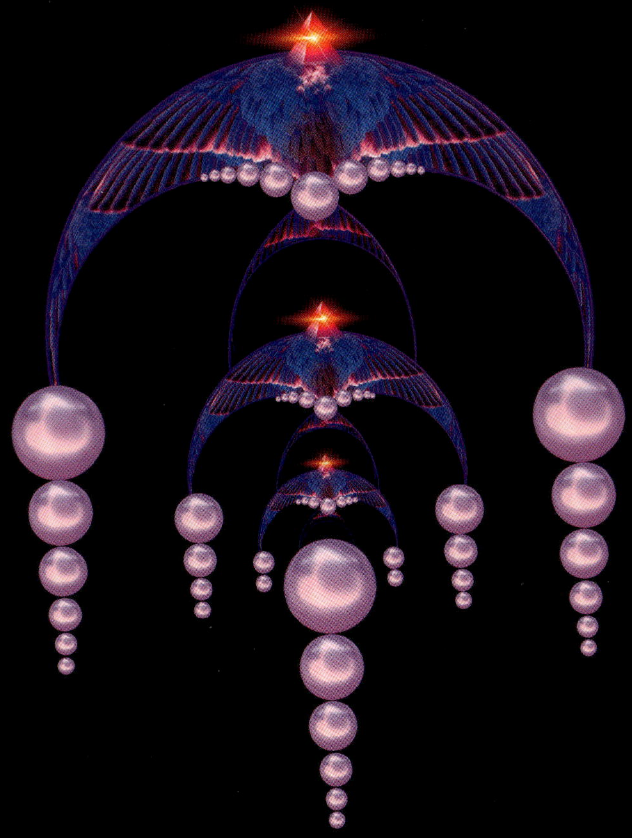

The life cycle XIX

Transition

inner space

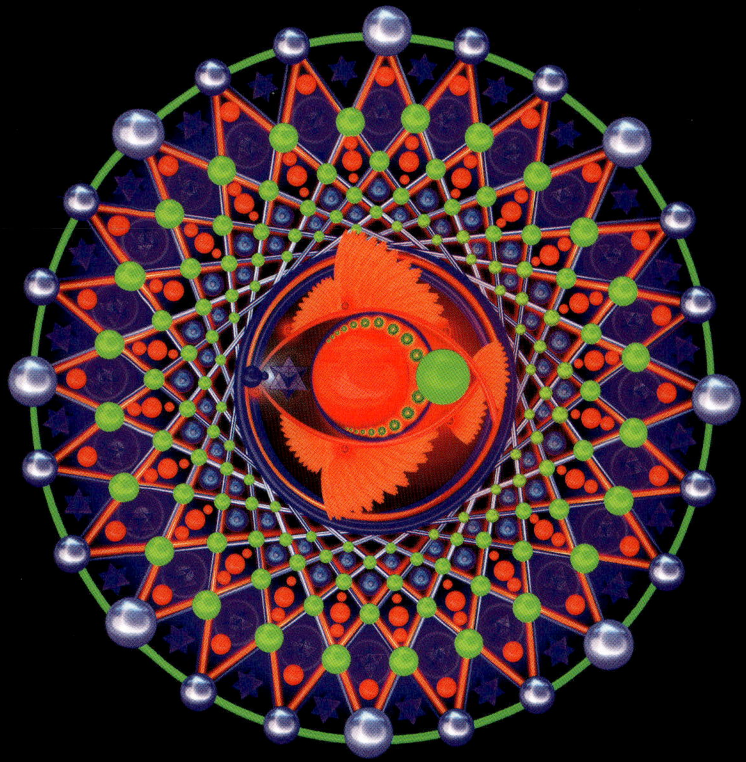

The life cycle XX

Development

inner space

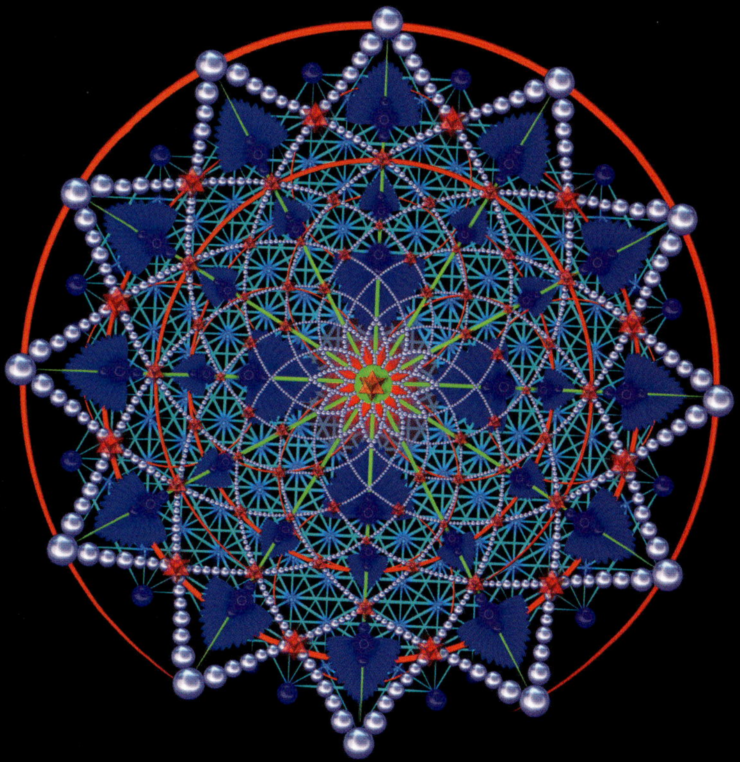

The life cycle XXI
Calling

inner space

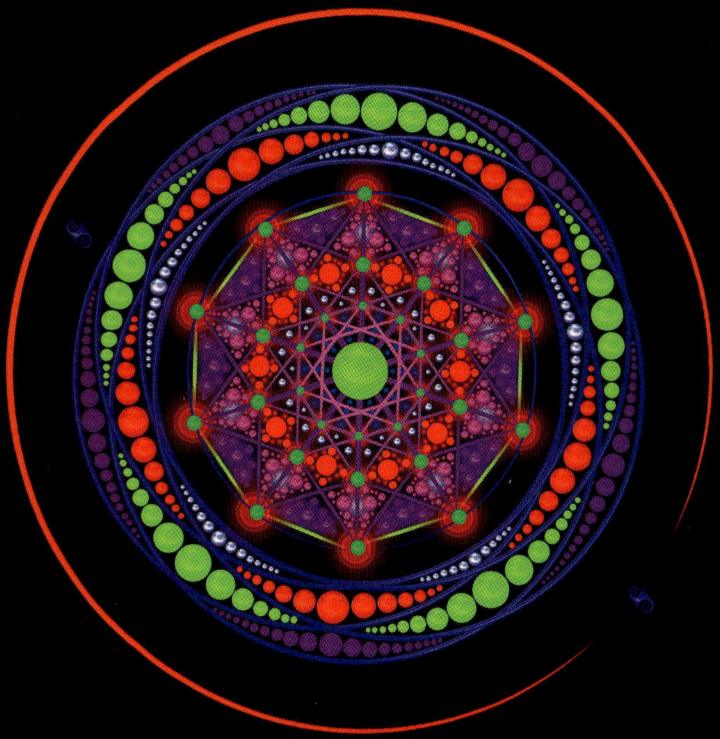

The life cycle XXII

Unity consciousness

inner space

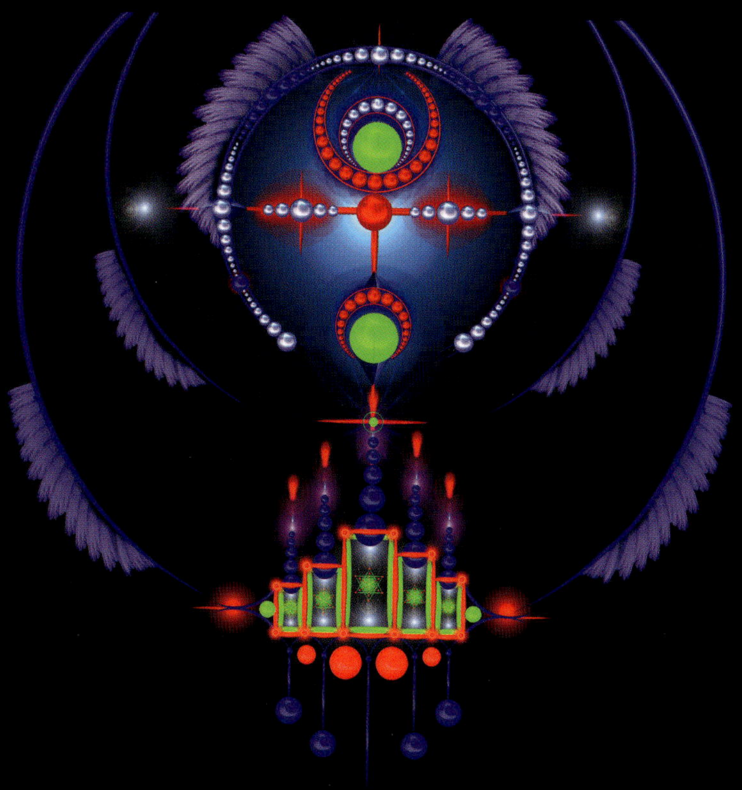

Growth & strength I

Natural time

inner space

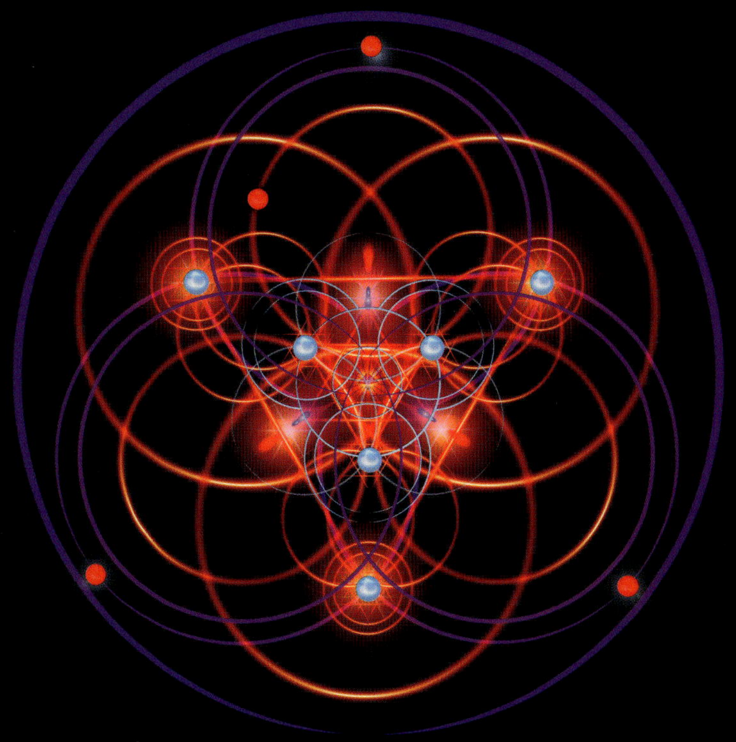

Growth & strength II

Empowerment

inner space

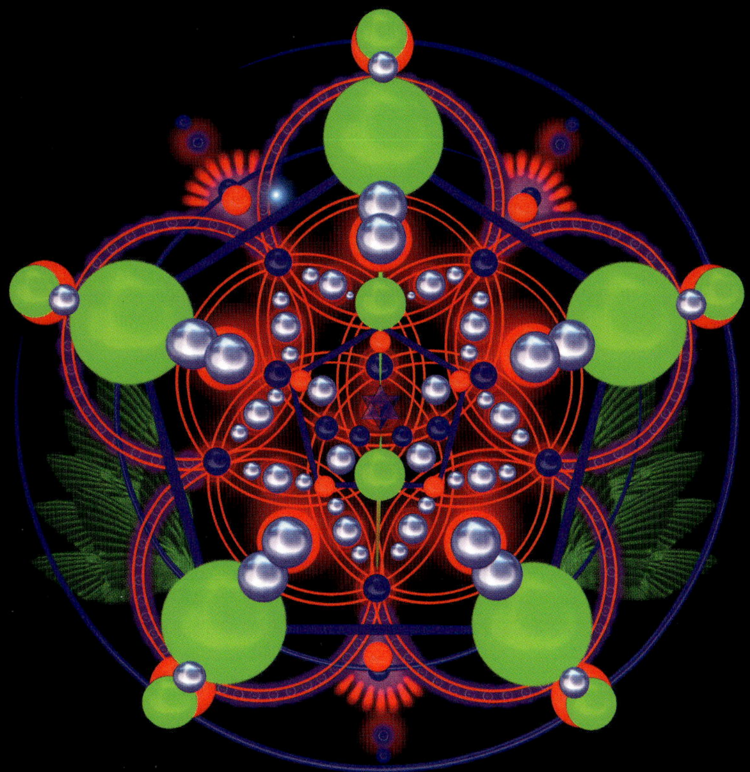

Growth & strength III

Imprint

inner space

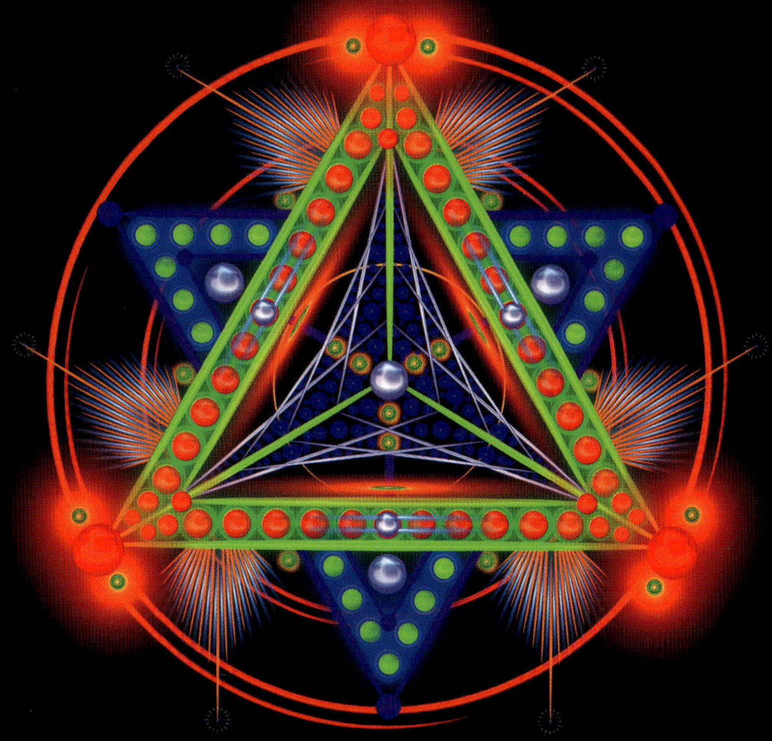

Growth & strength IV
Victory

inner space

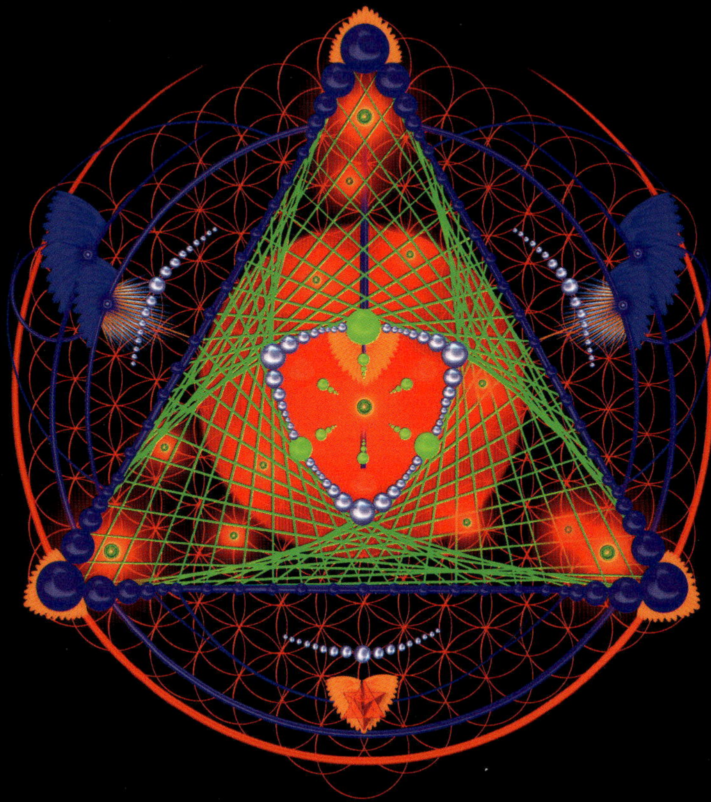

Growth & strength V

Rescue

inner space

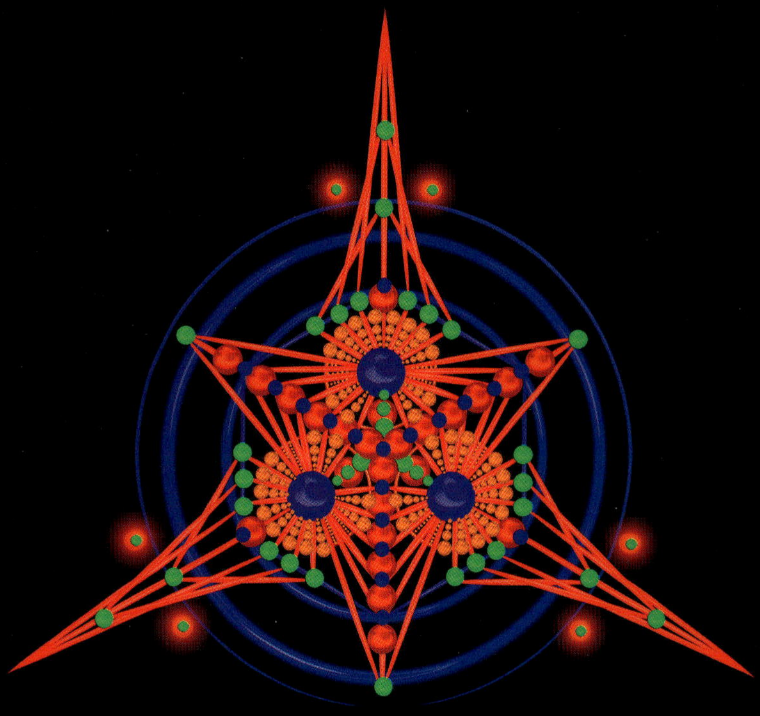

Growth & strength VI
Transfiguration

inner space

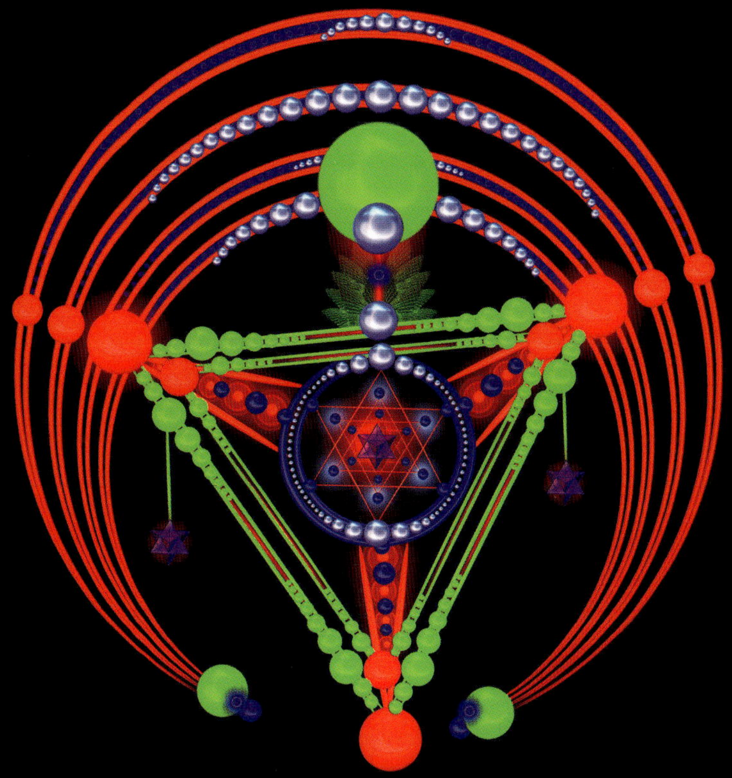

Growth & strength VII

Perspective

inner space

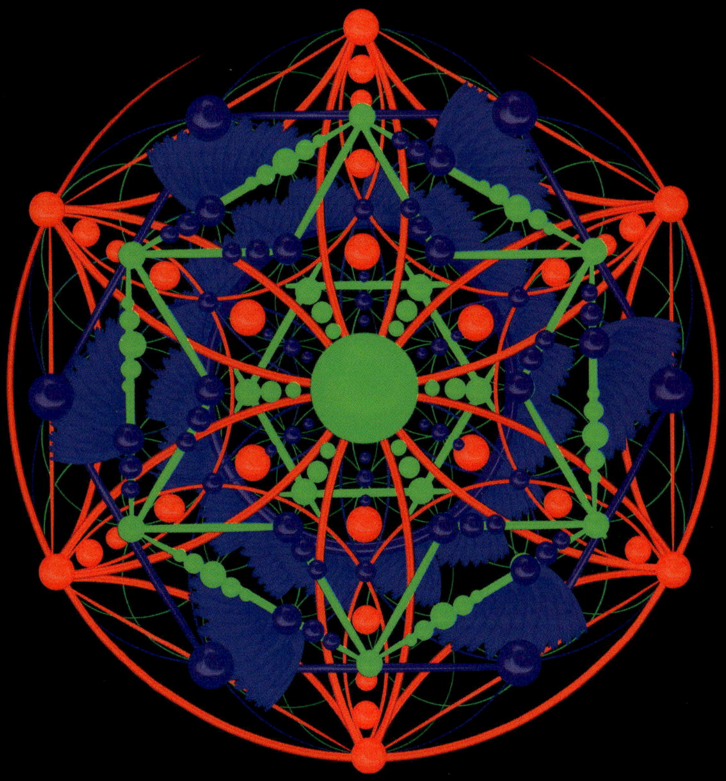

Growth & strength VIII

Momentum

inner space

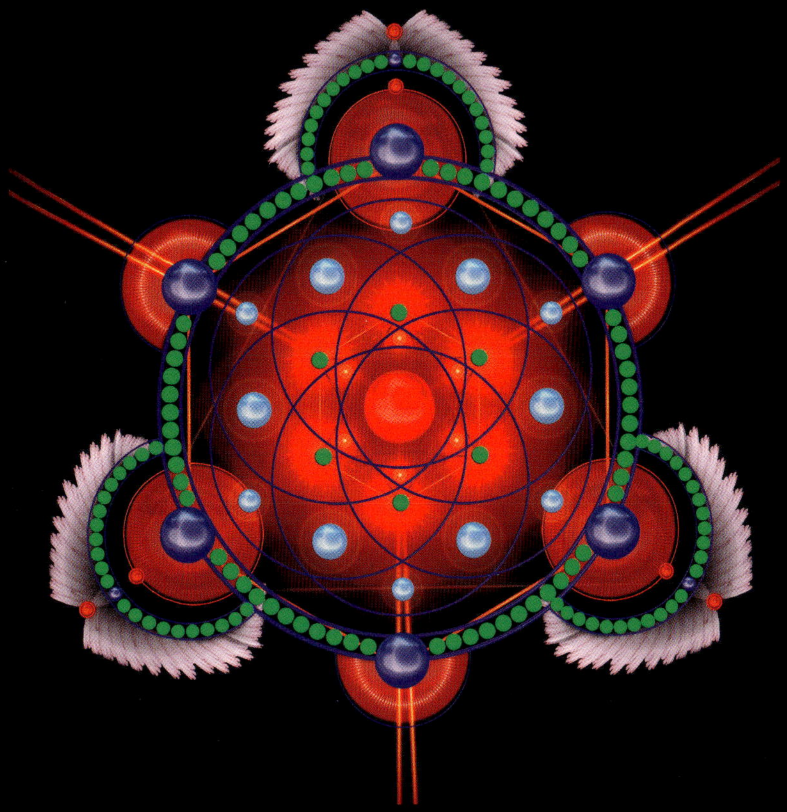

Growth & strength IX
Resistance

inner space

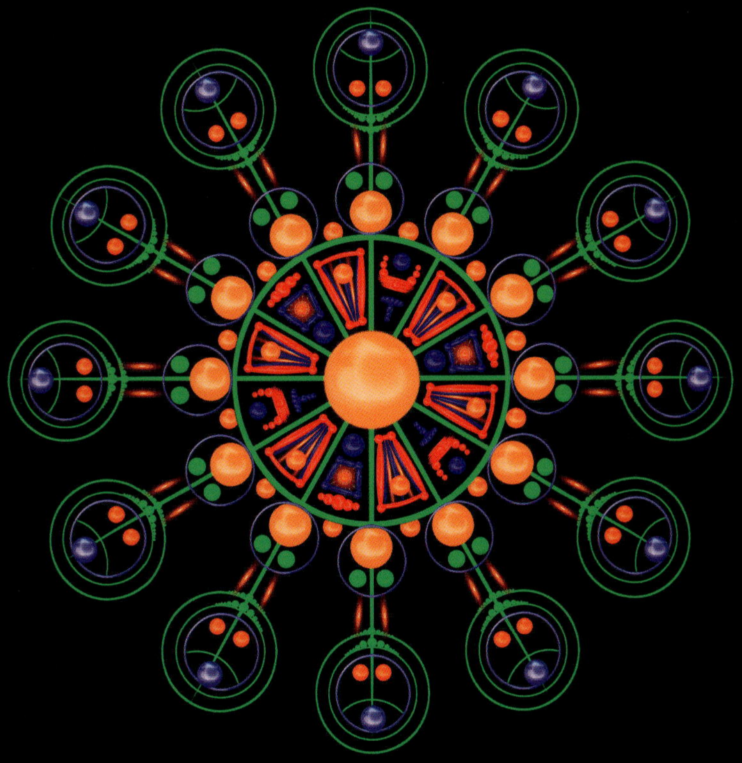

Growth & strength X
Repetition

inner space

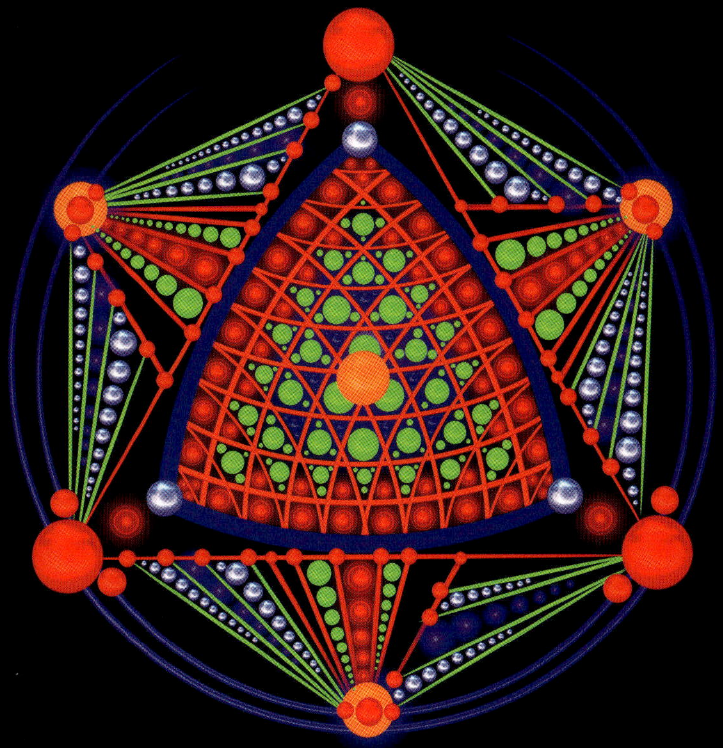

Growth & strength XI

Joining

inner space

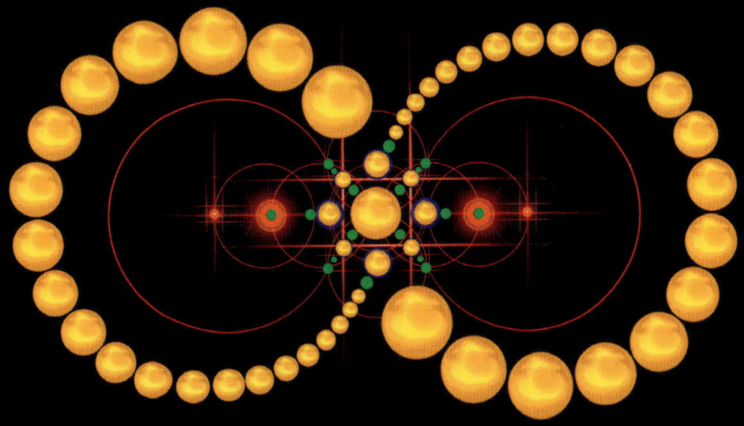

Growth & strength XII

Protection

inner space

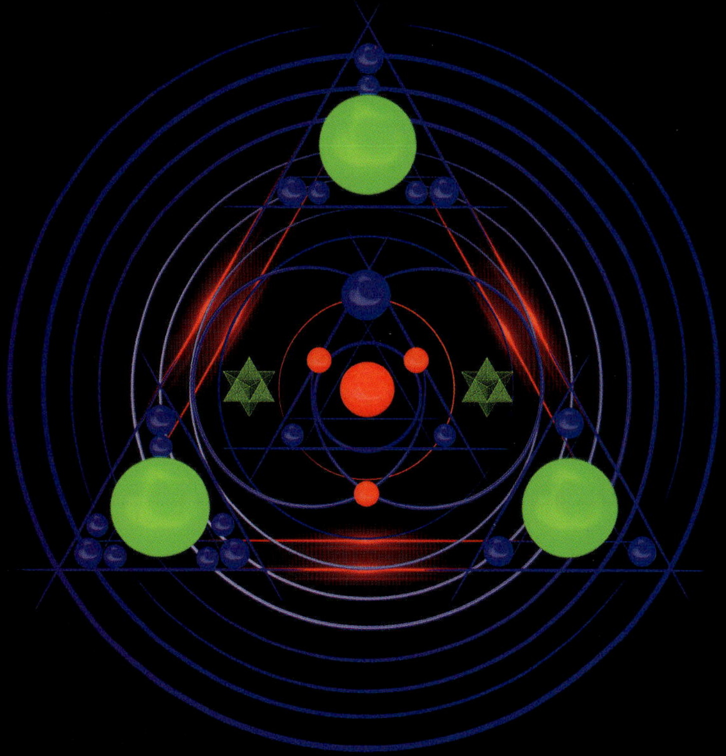

Growth & strength XIII

Balance

inner space

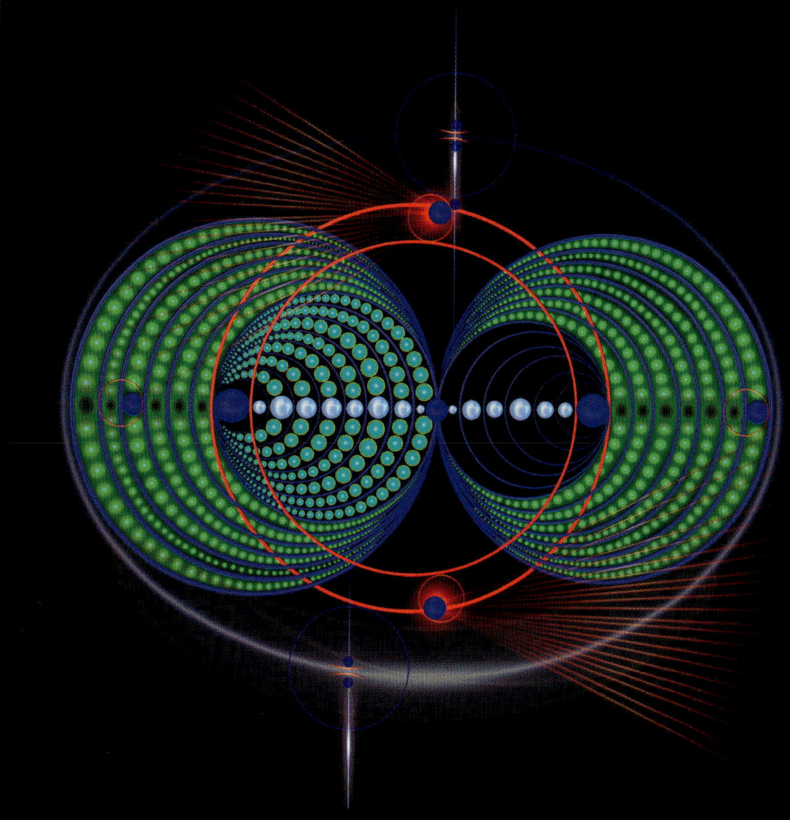

Growth & strength XIV
Trust

inner space

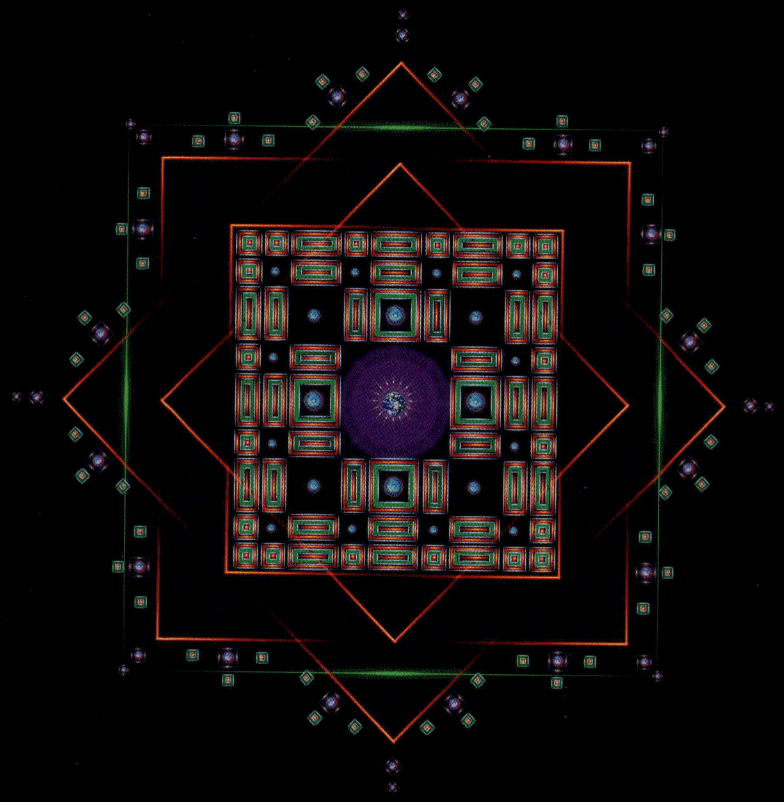

The art of creation I

Manifestation

inner space

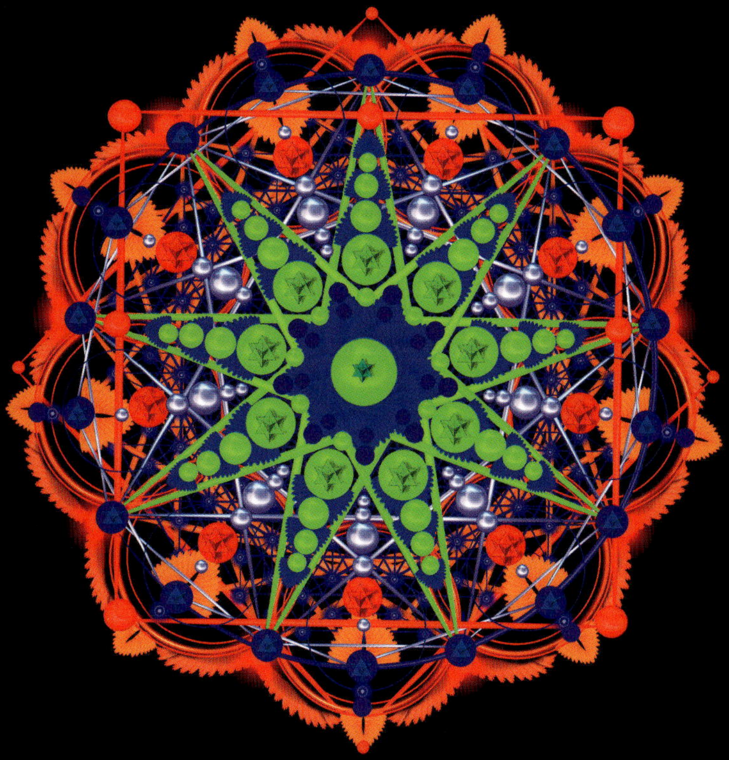

The art of creation II
Perseverance

inner space

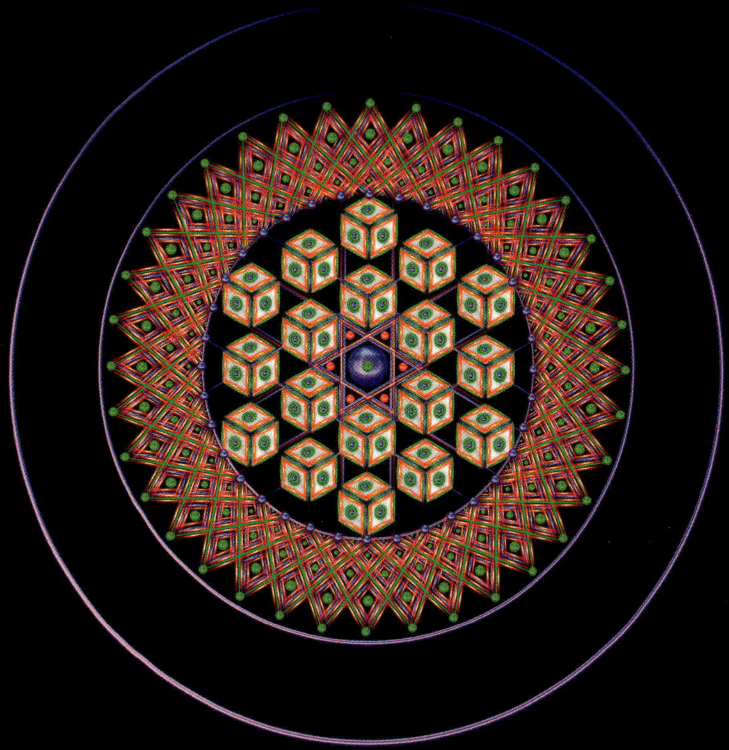

The art of creation III

Transformation

inner space

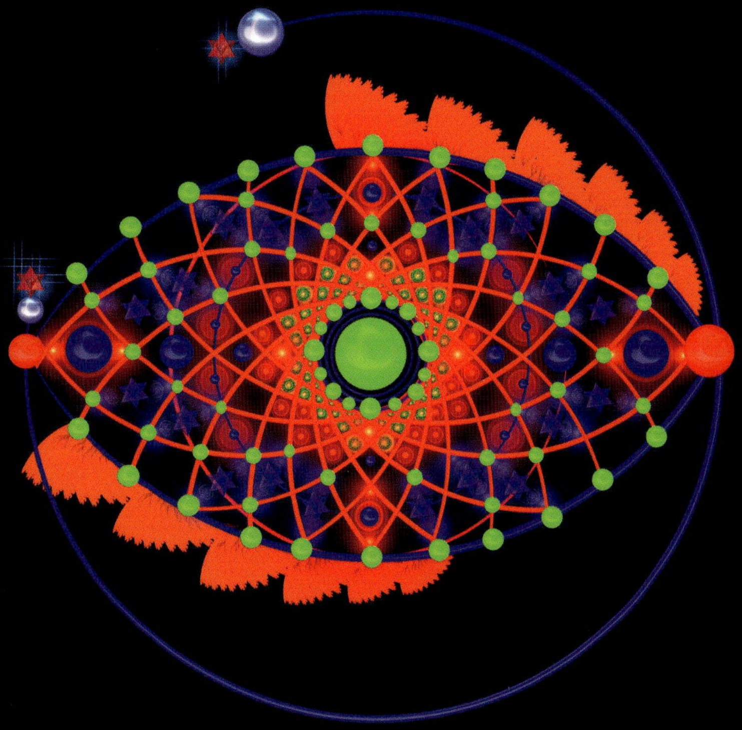

The art of creation IV

Processing

inner space

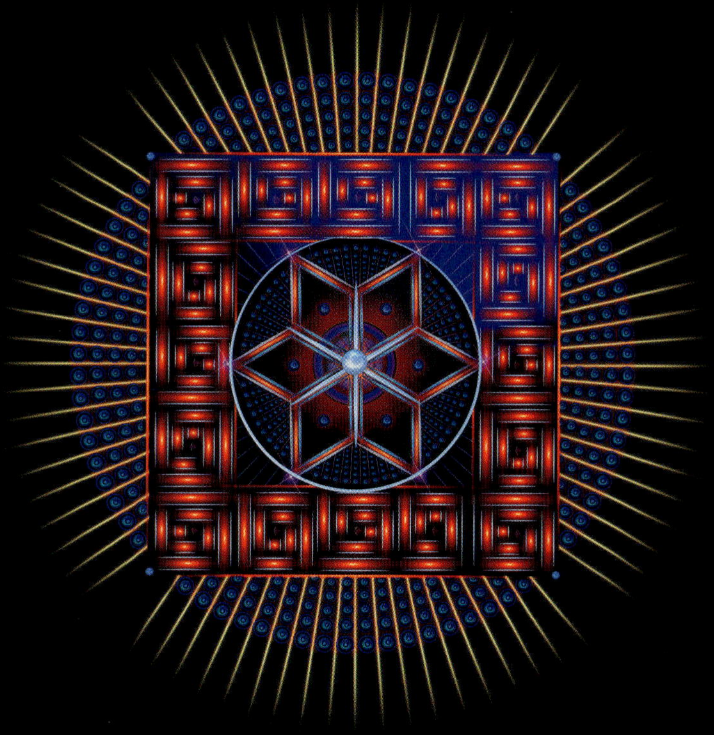

The art of creation V

Self-confidence

inner space

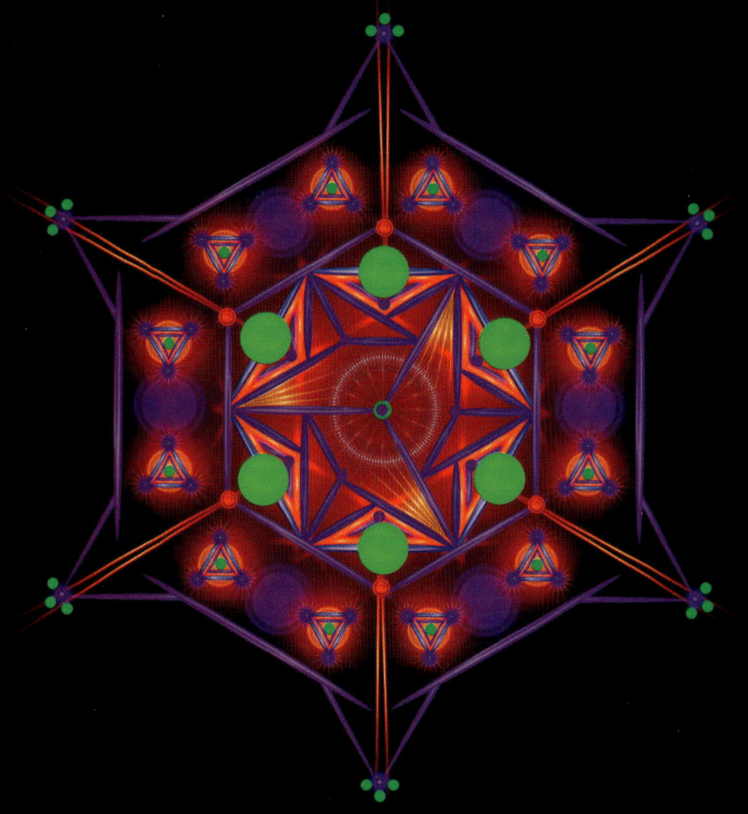

The art of creation VI
Direction

inner space

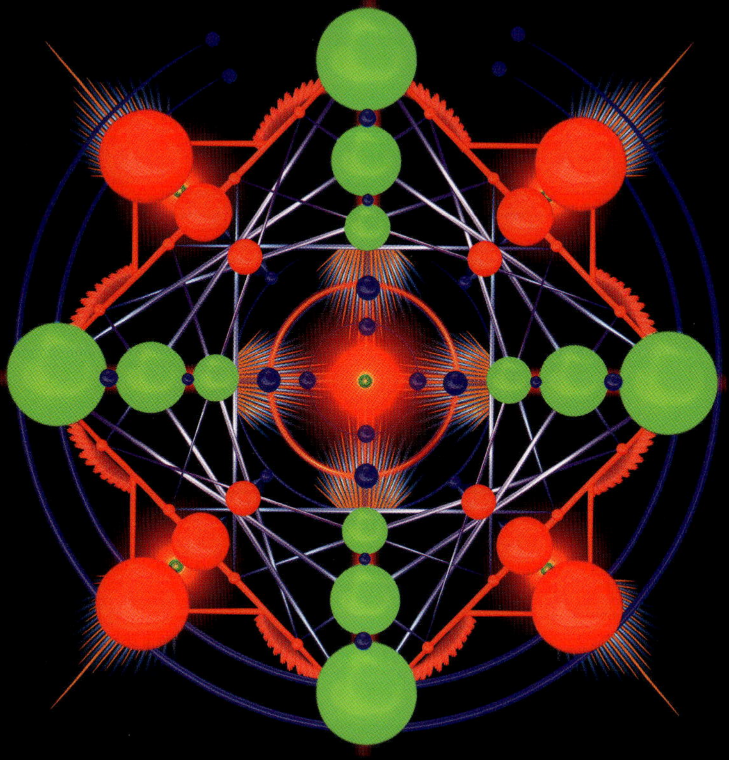

The art of creation VII

Resilience

inner space

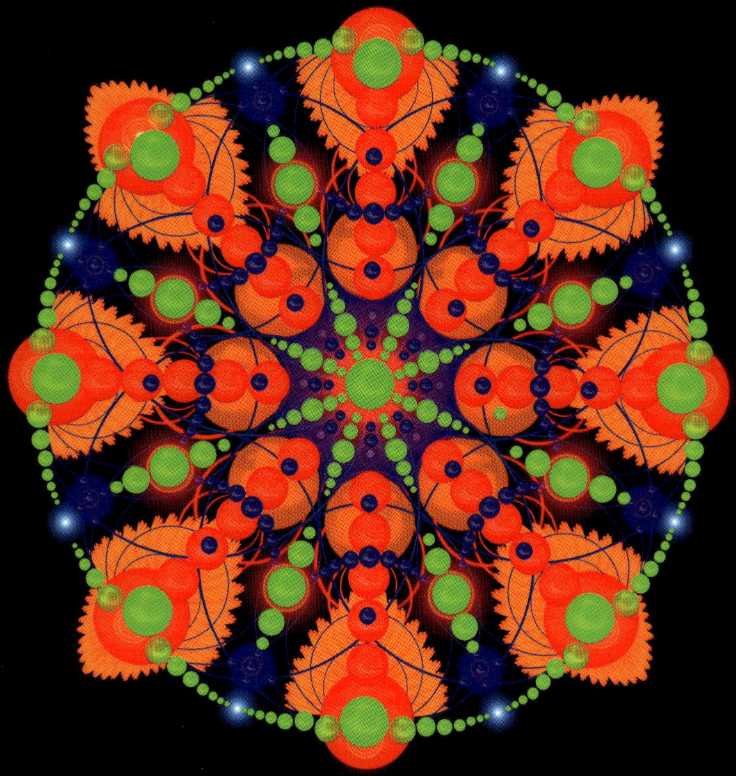

The art of creation VIII
Focus

inner space

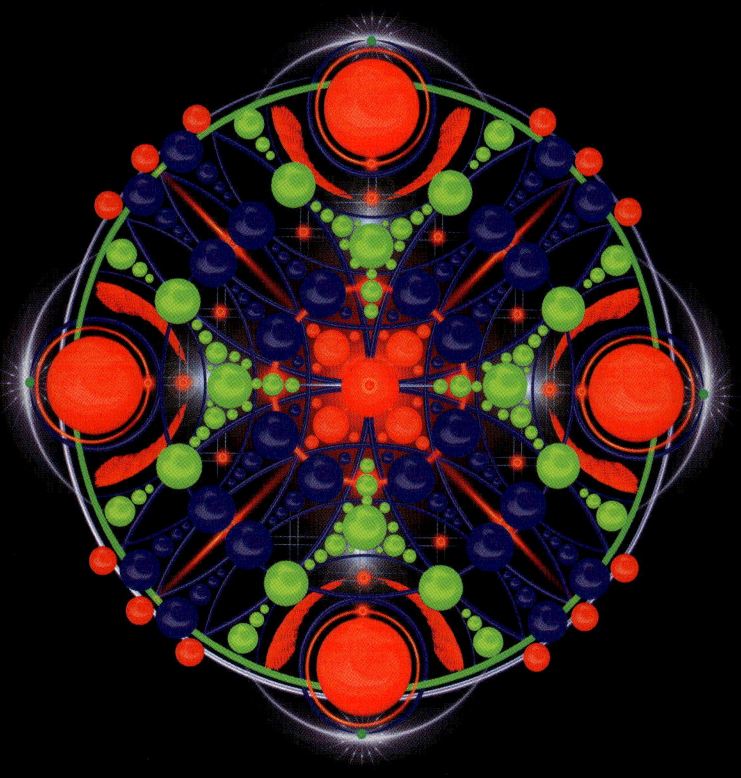

The art of creation IX

Coming home

inner space

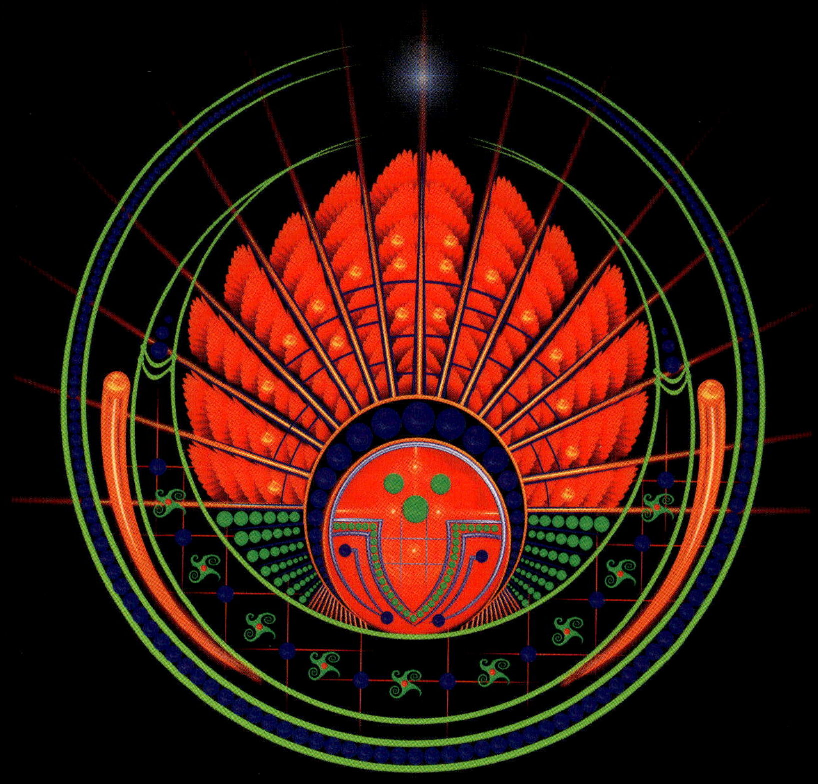

The art of creation X

Breakthrough

inner space

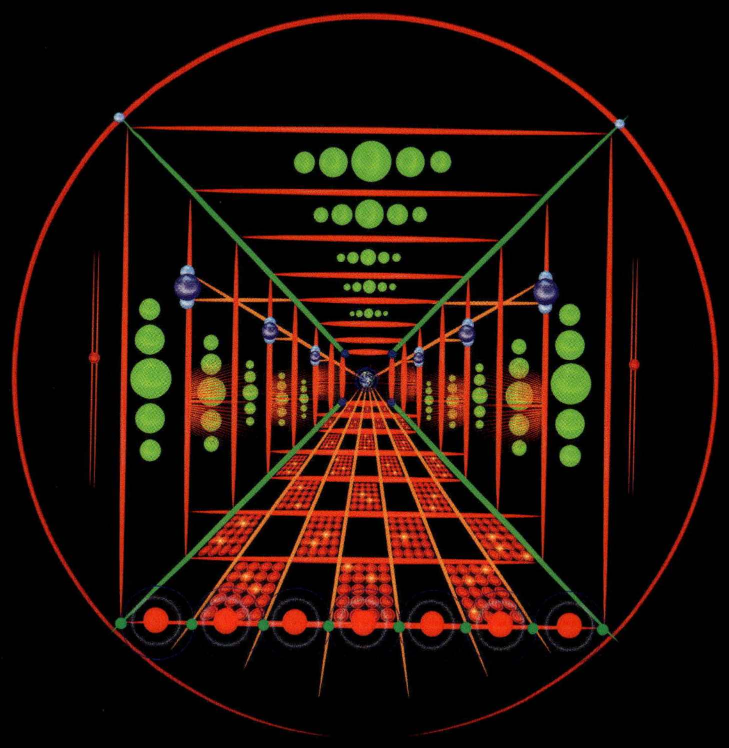

The art of creation XI

Opportunities

inner space

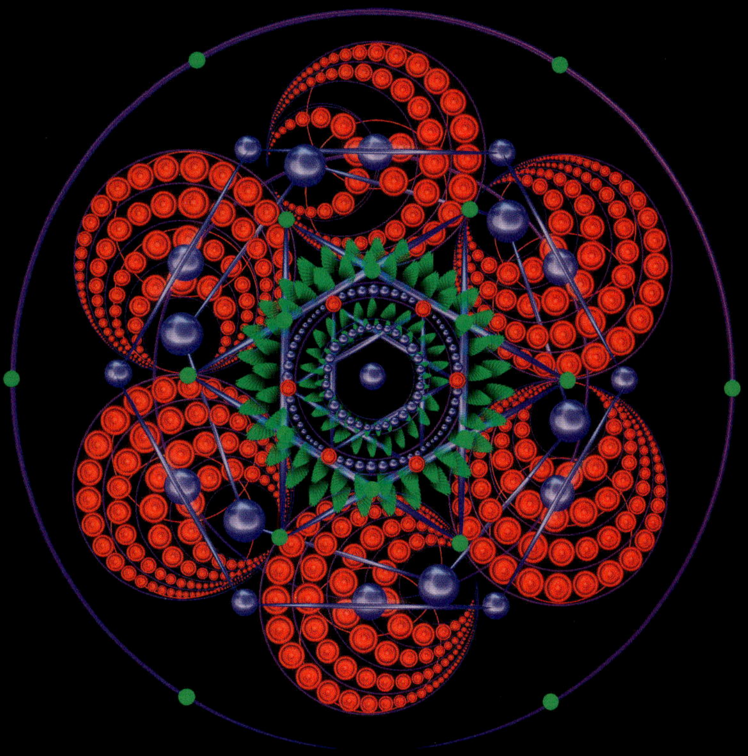

The art of creation XII

Completeness

inner space

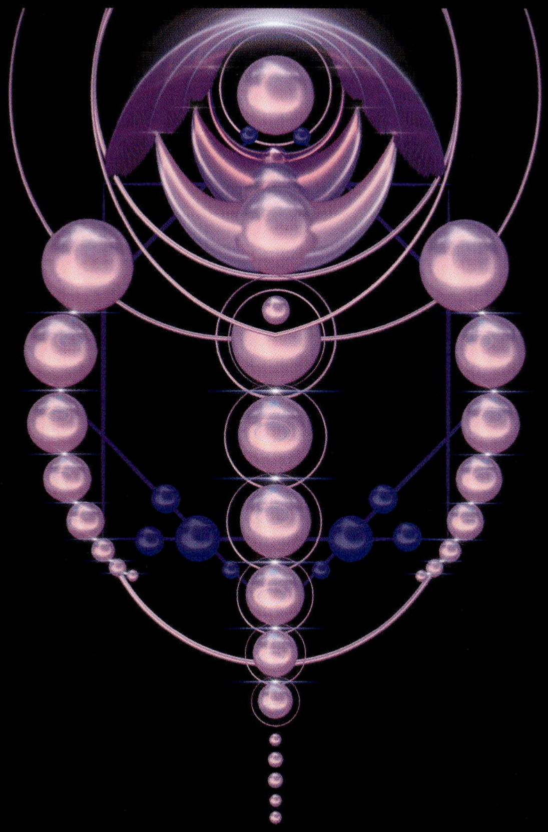

The art of creation XIII

Emergence

inner space

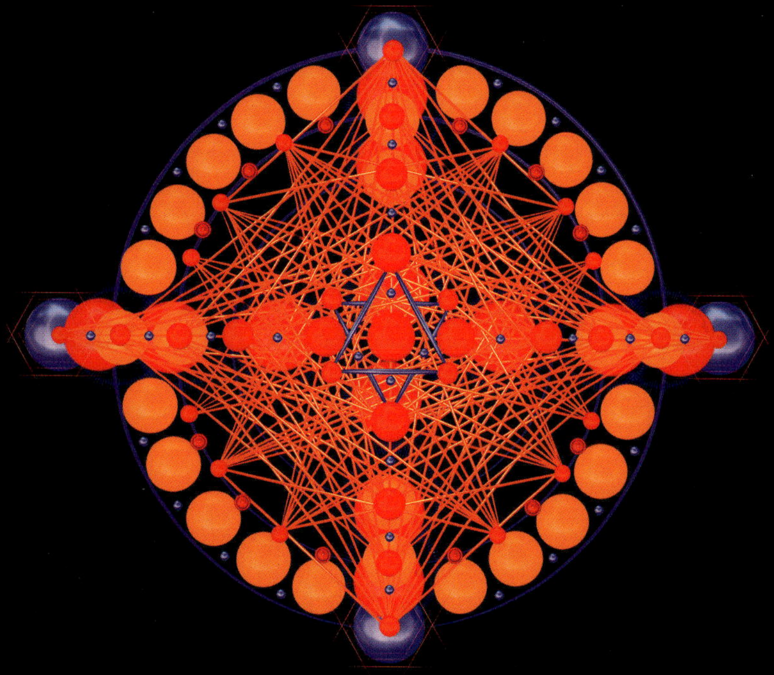

The art of creation XIV

Knowledge

inner space

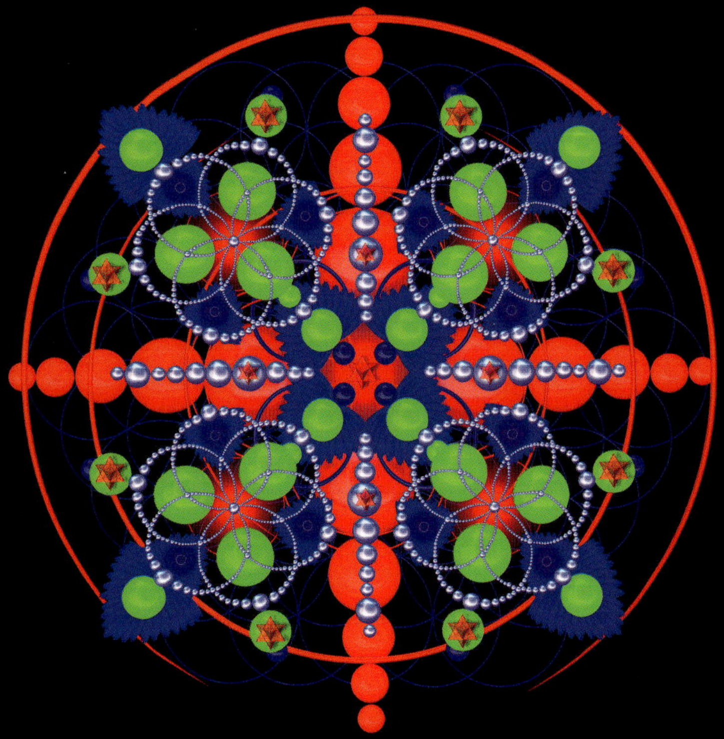

From knowledge to wisdom I

Essence

inner space

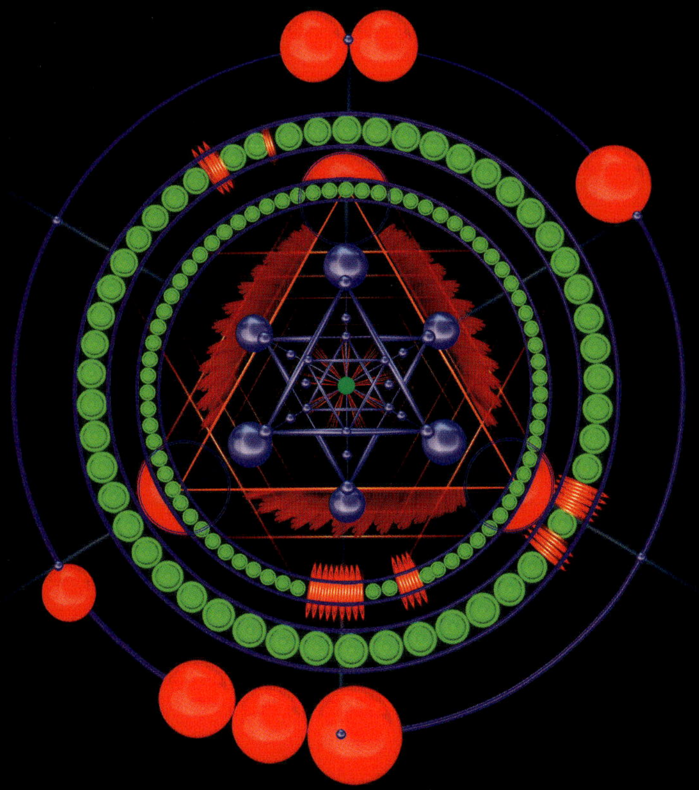

From knowledge to wisdom II
Awareness

inner space

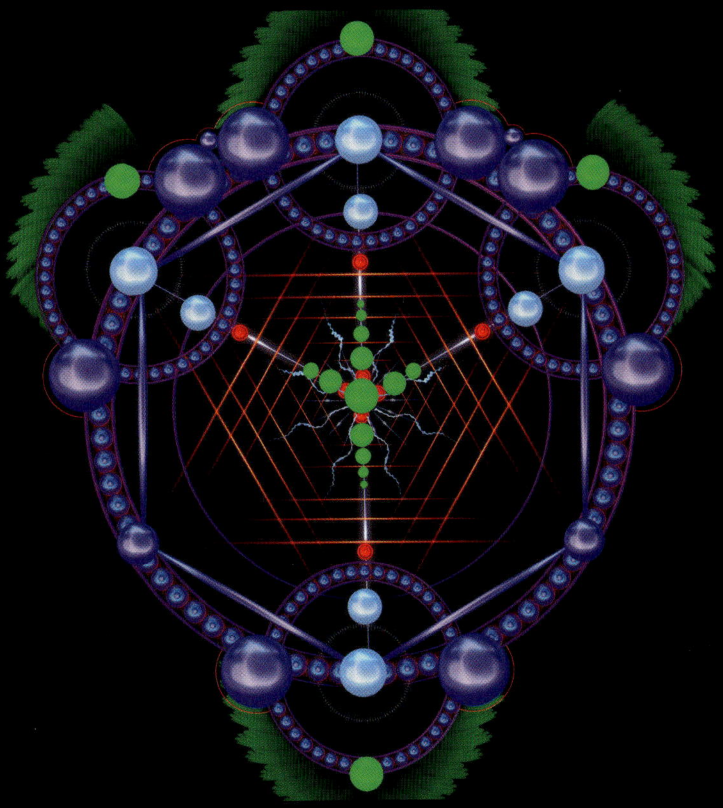

From knowledge to wisdom III
Compassion

inner space

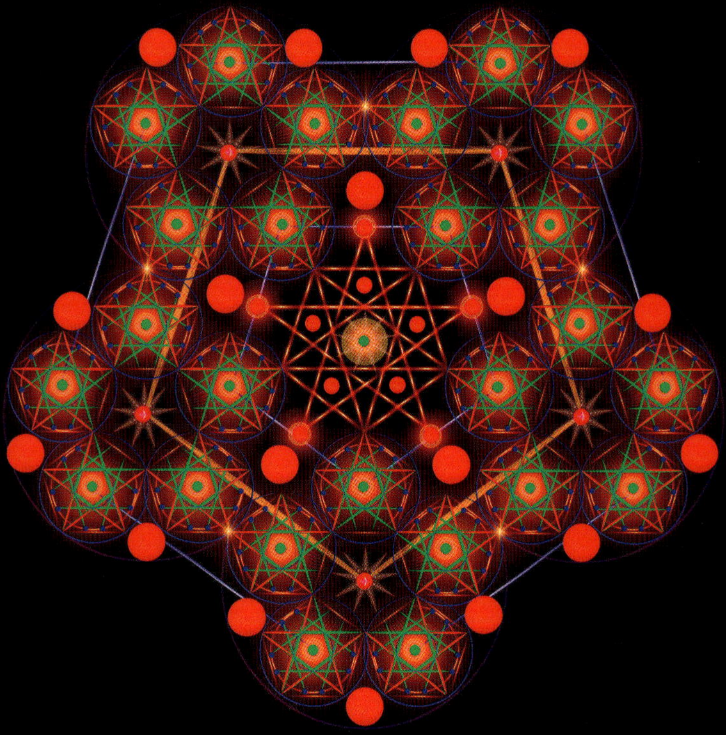

From knowledge to wisdom IV

Self-reflection

inner space

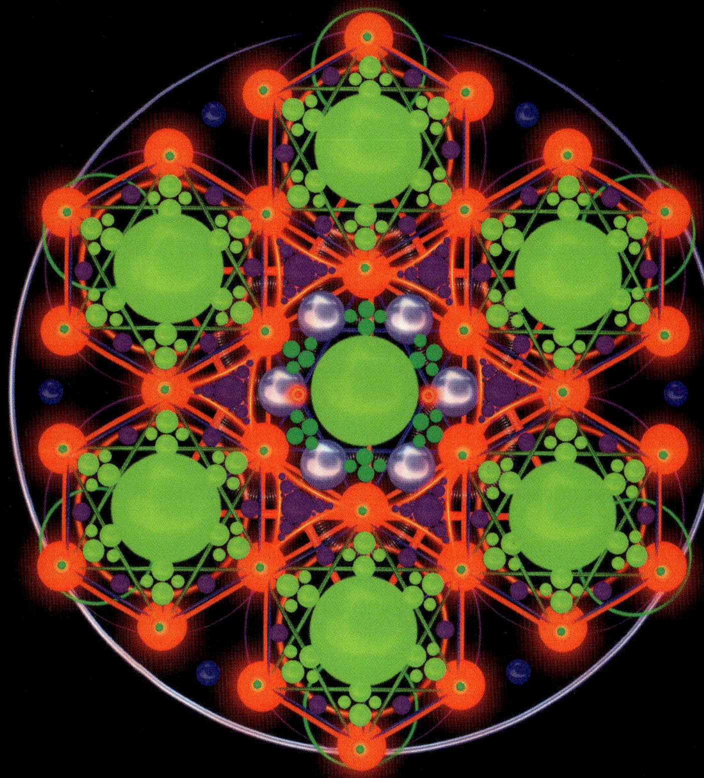

From knowledge to wisdom V

Newborn time

inner space

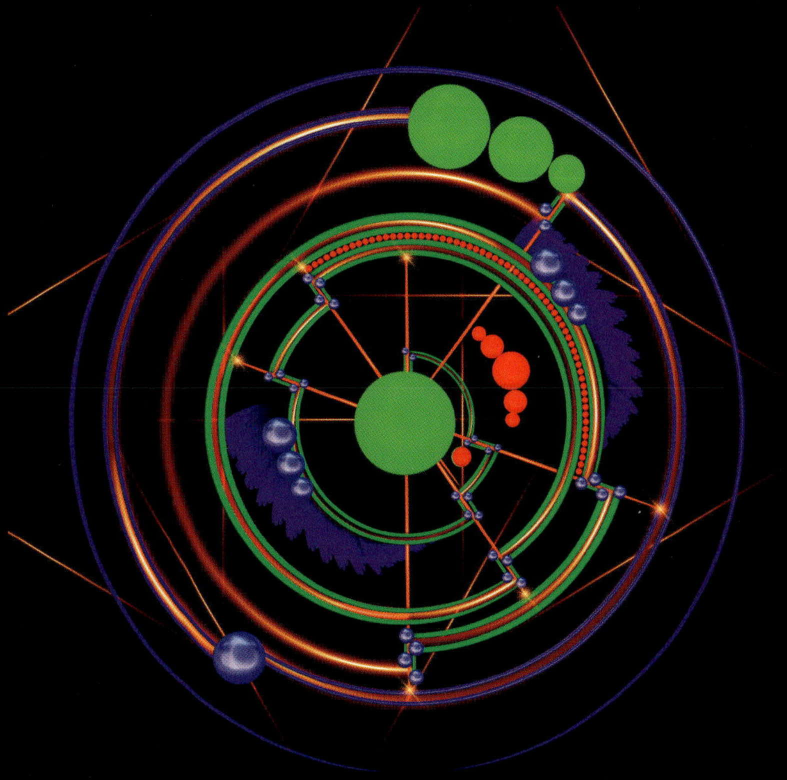

From knowledge to wisdom VI

Shifting

inner space

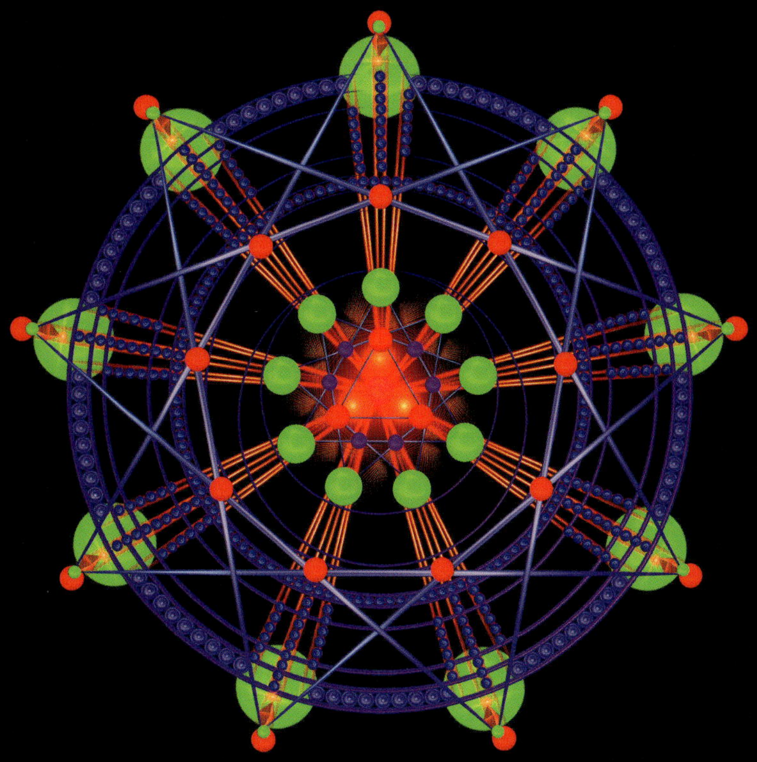

From knowledge to wisdom VII
Choices

inner space

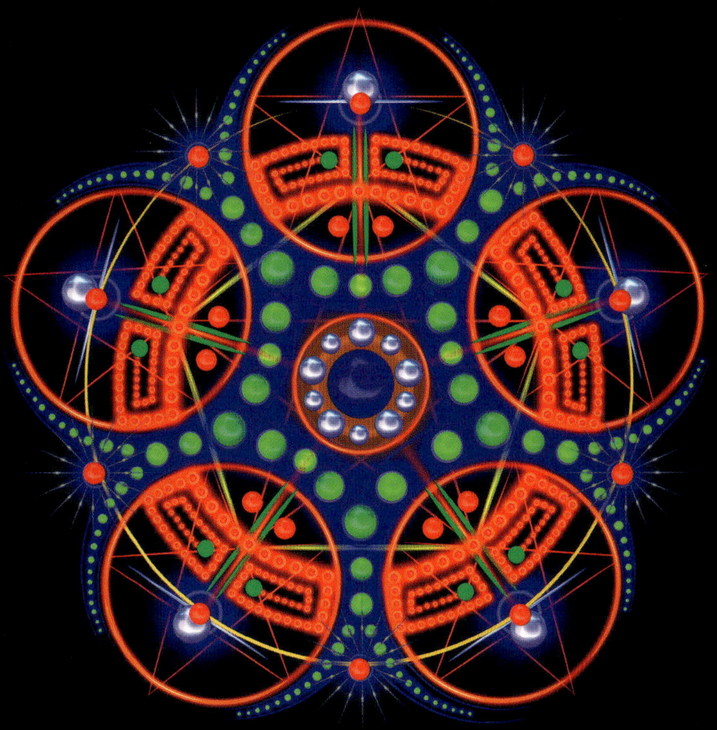

From knowledge to wisdom VIII

Life plan

inner space

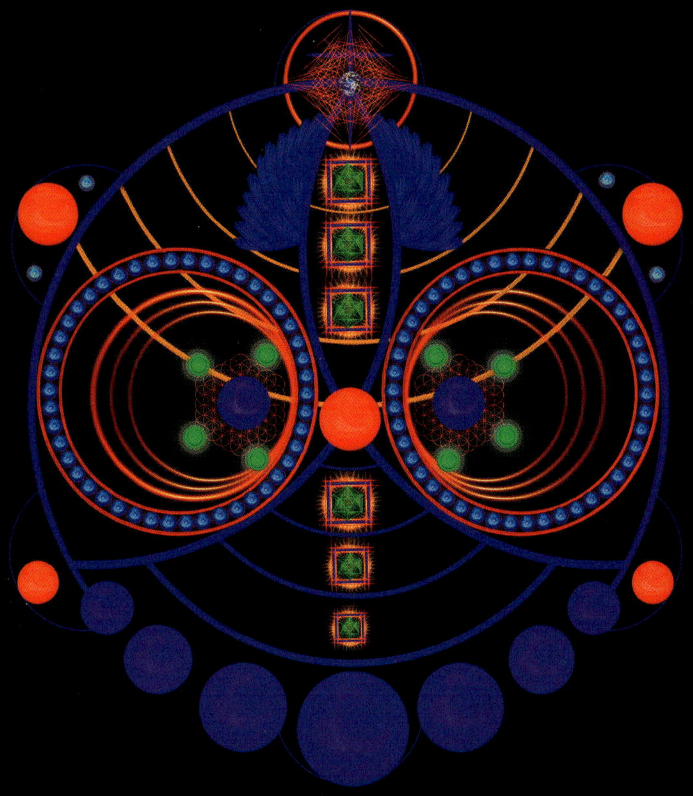

From knowledge to wisdom X

Communication

inner space

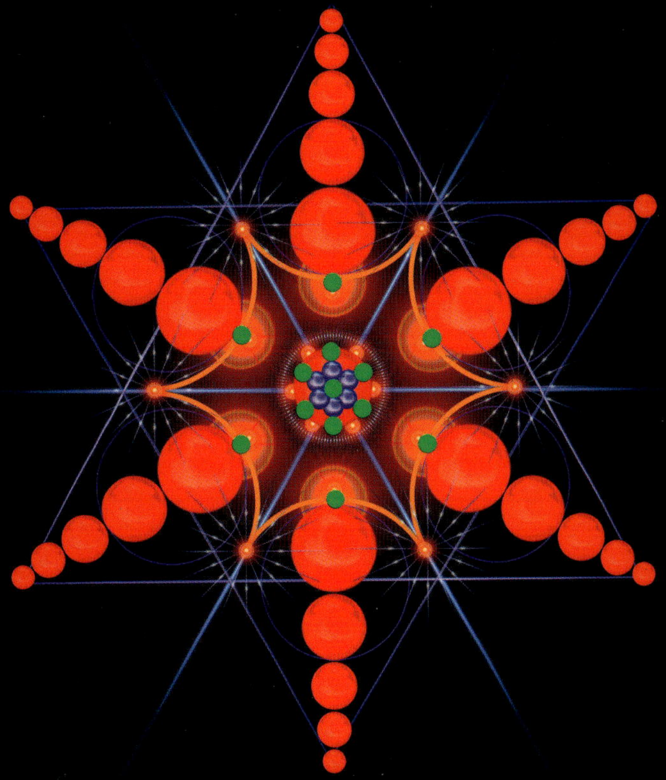

From knowledge to wisdom XI

Acceptance

inner space

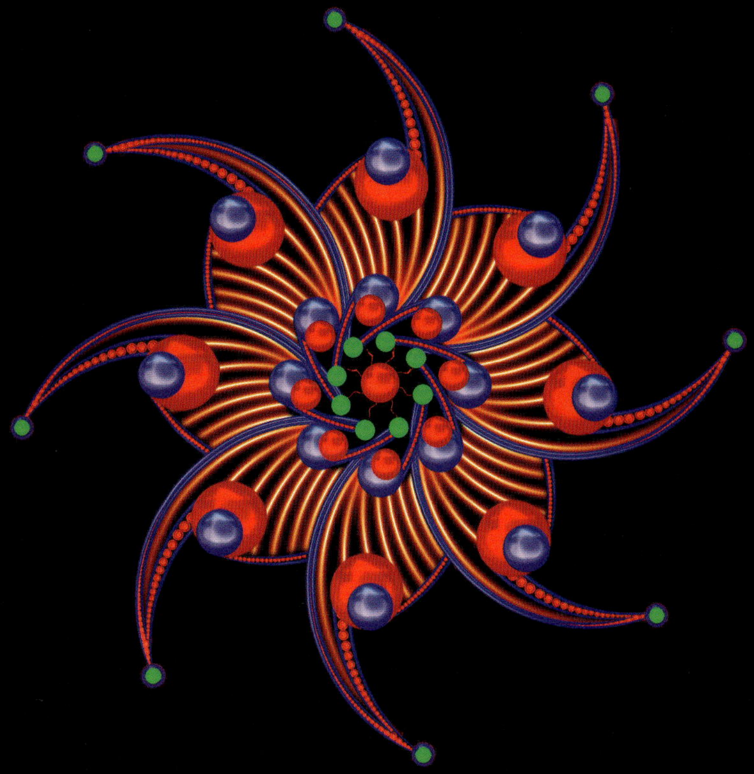

From knowledge to wisdom XII
Purity

inner space

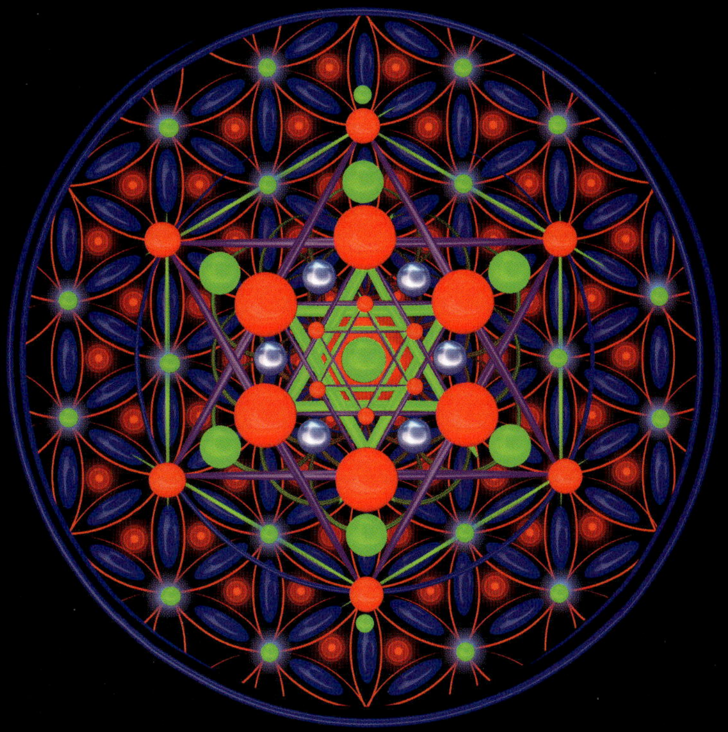

From knowledge to wisdom XIII
Talent

inner space

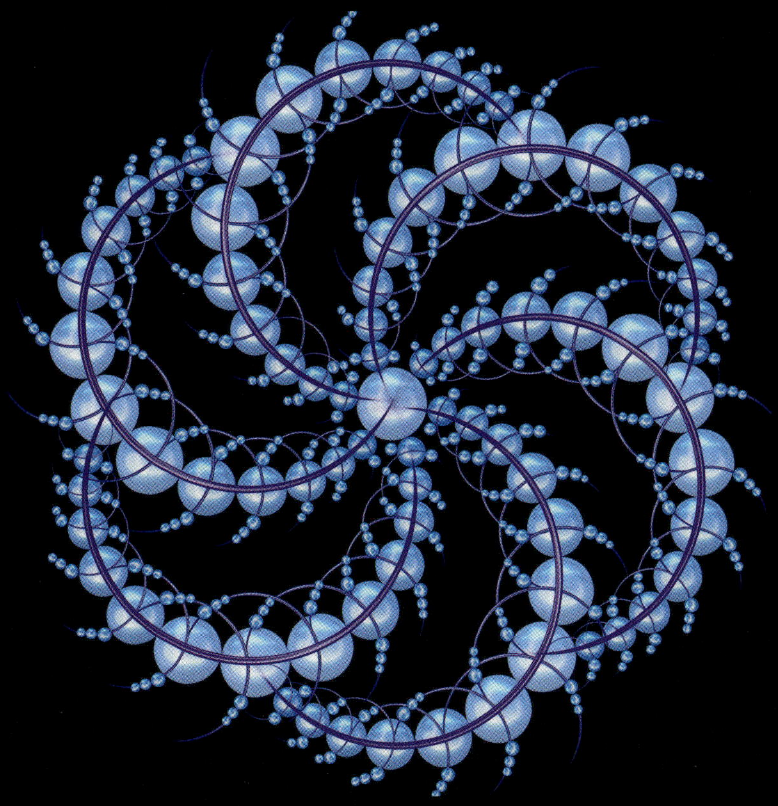

From knowledge to wisdom XIV

Confirmation

inner space

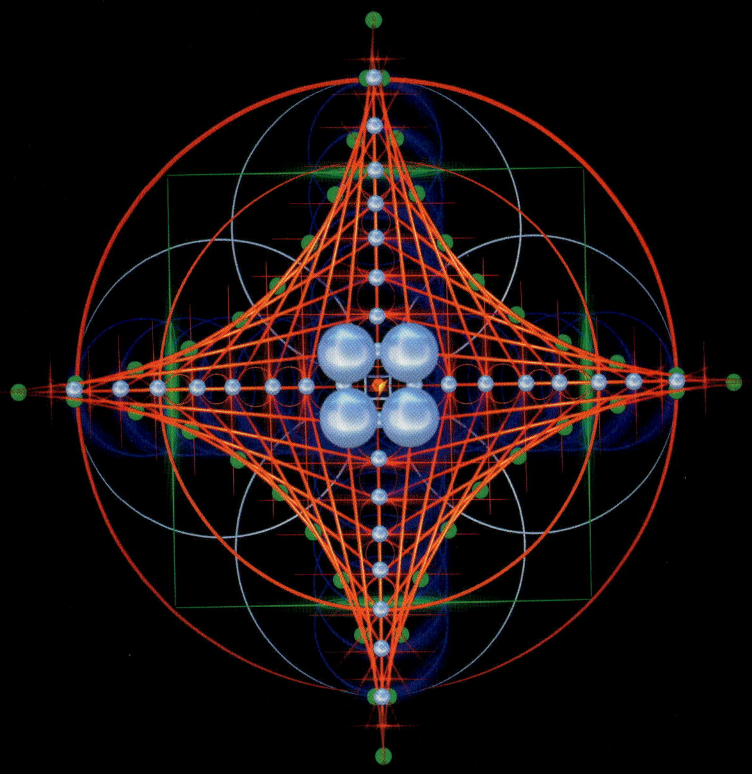

Unconditional love I
Security

inner space

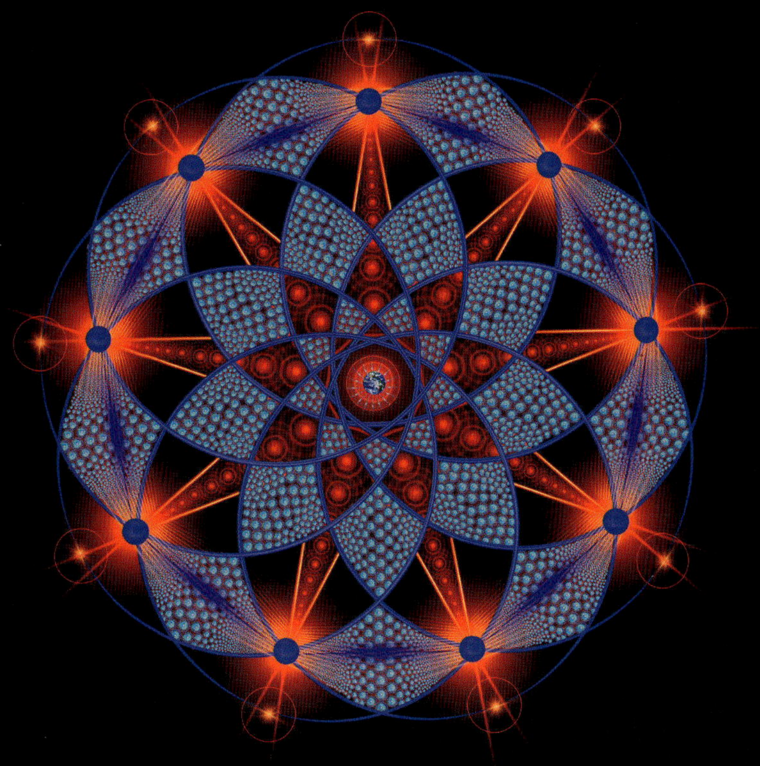

Unconditional love II
Unconditionality

inner space

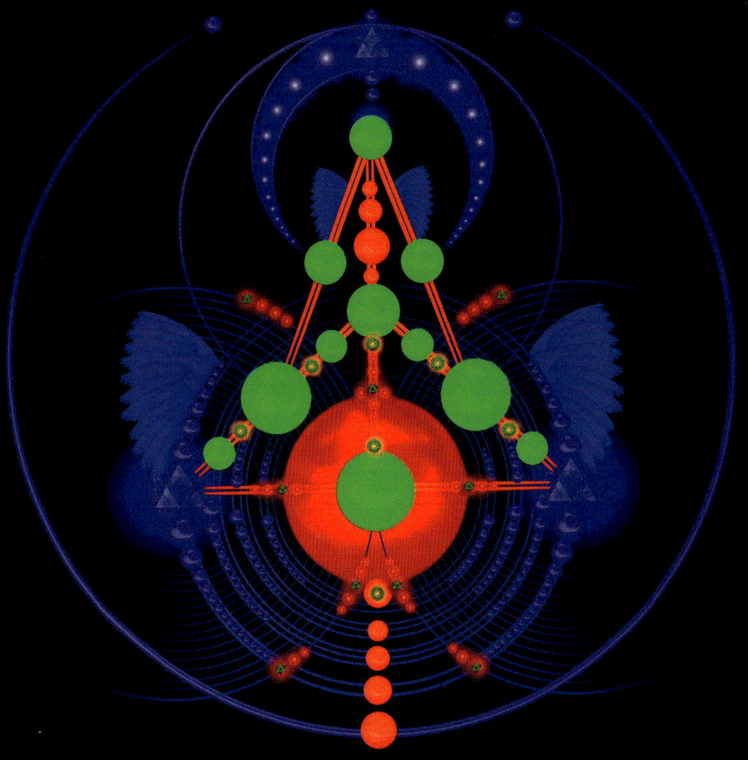

Unconditional love III
Satisfaction

inner space

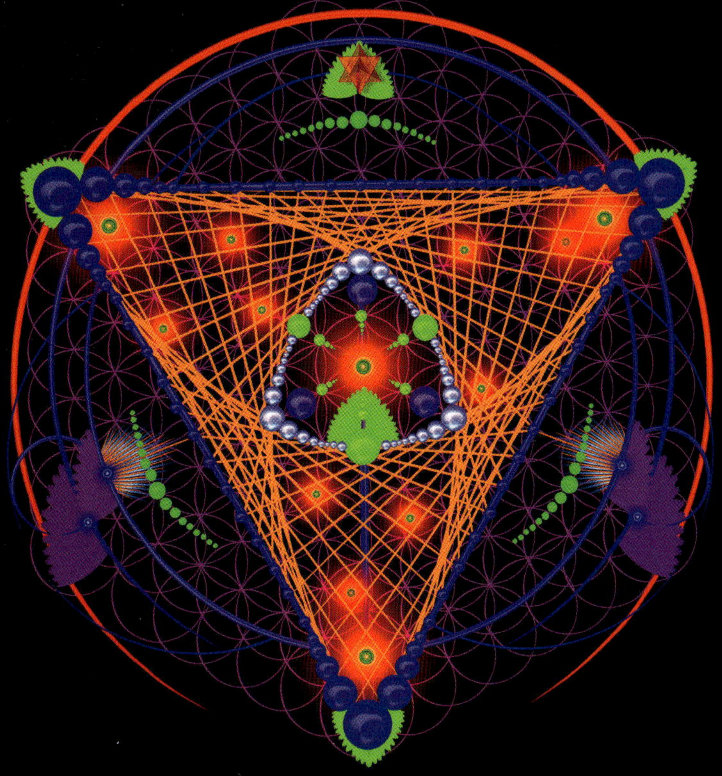

Unconditional love IV

Disconnecting

inner space

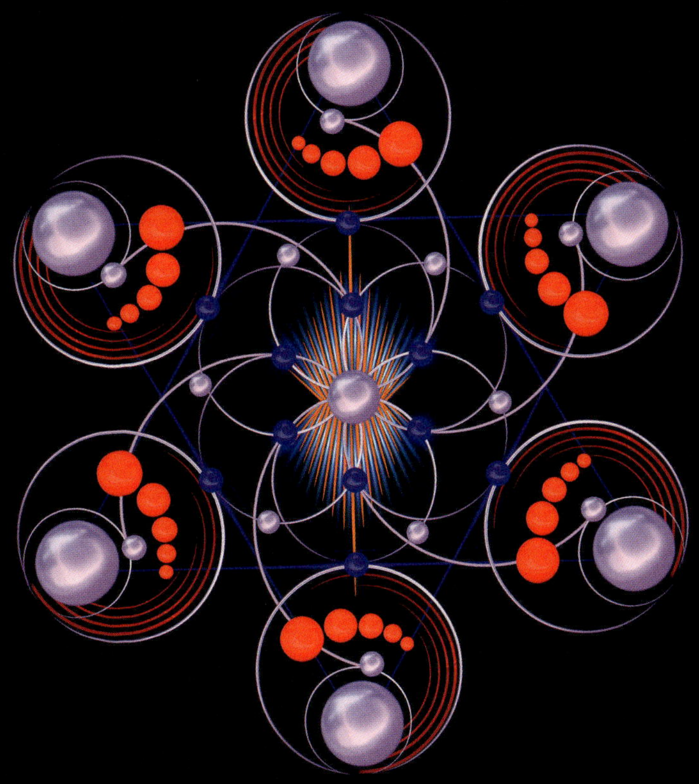

Unconditional love V

Forgiveness

inner space

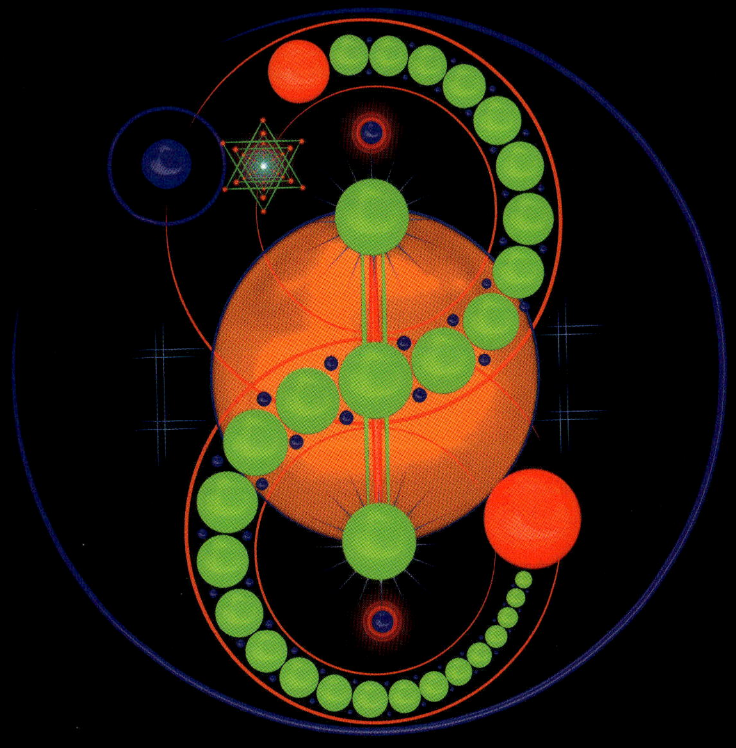

Unconditional love VI
Revelation

inner space

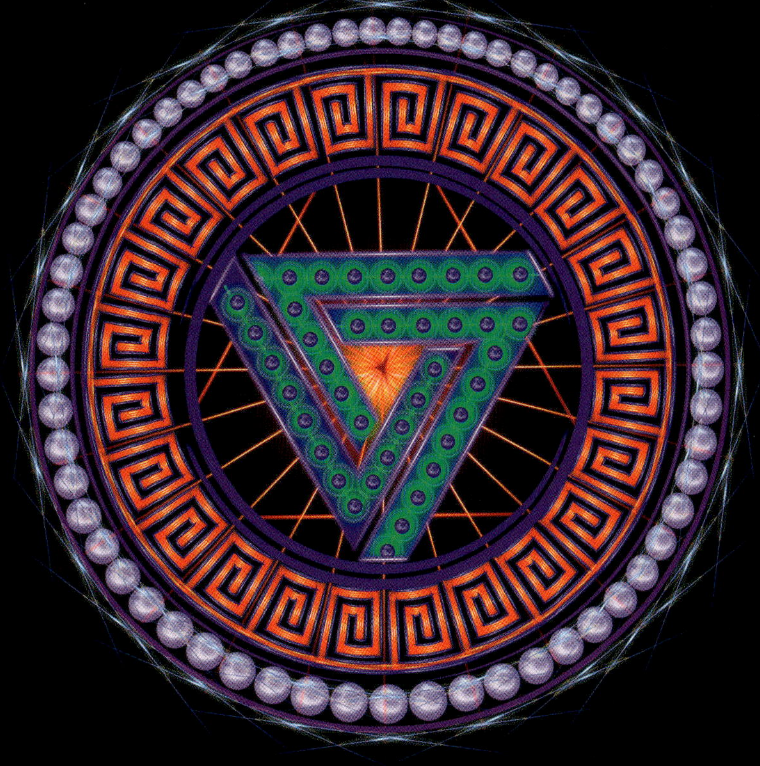

Unconditional love VII
Patience

inner space

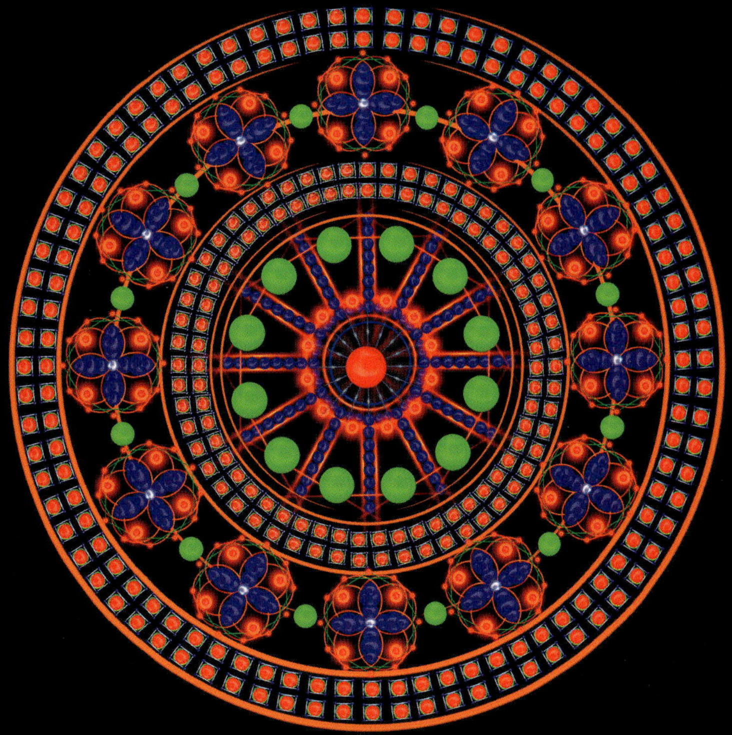

Unconditional love VIII

Desire

inner space

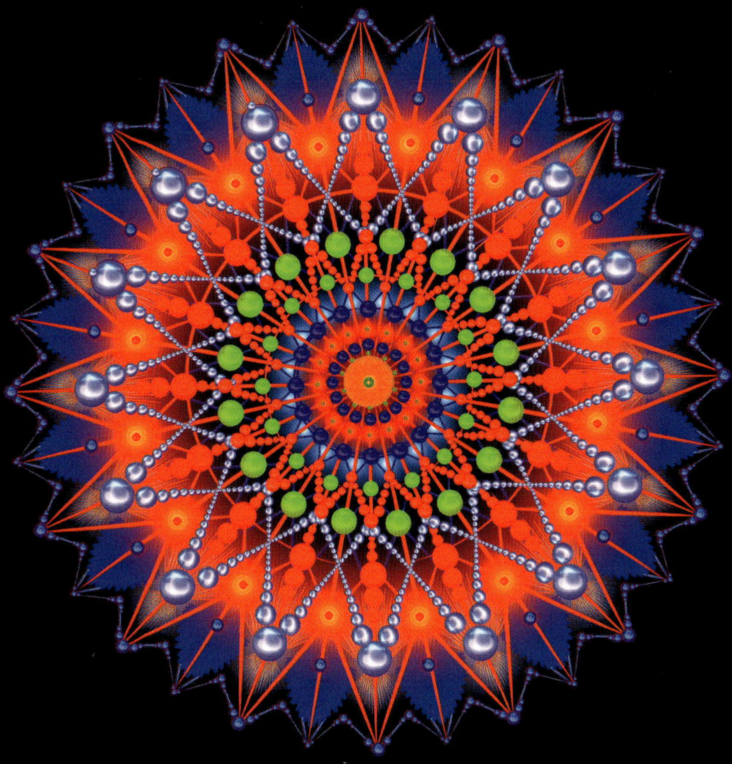

Unconditional love IX

Inner freedom

inner space

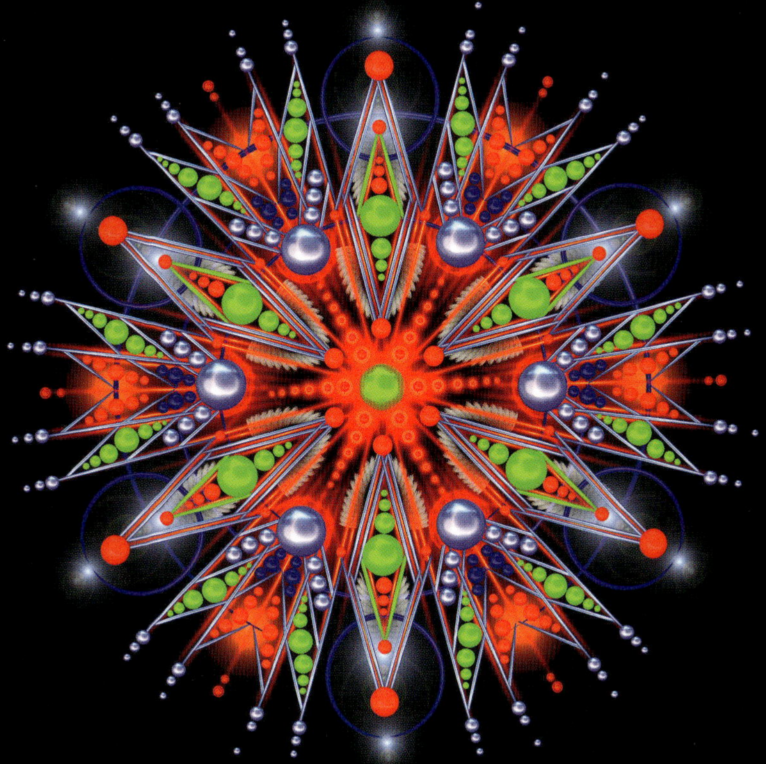

Unconditional love X
Sexuality

inner space

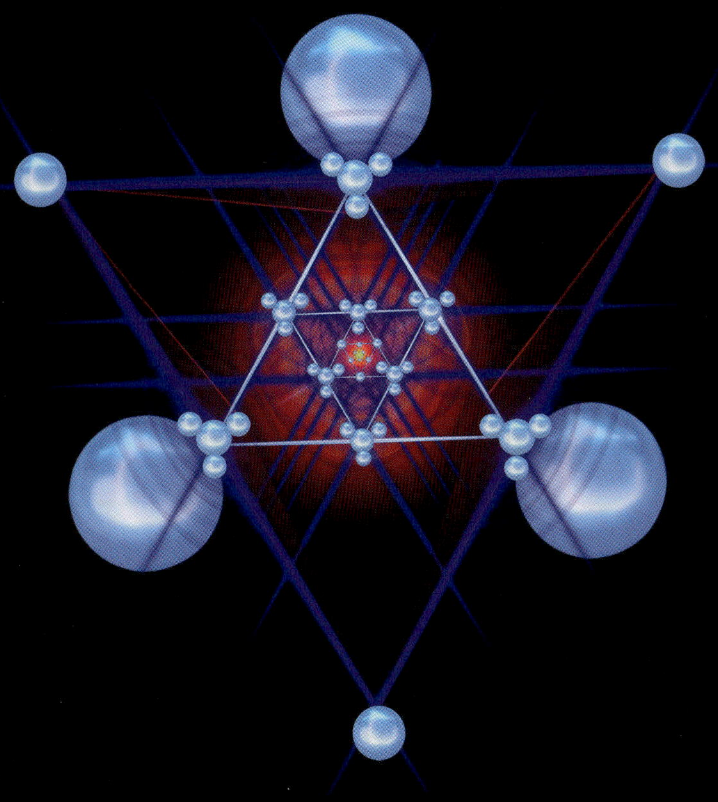

Unconditional love XI

Contact

inner space

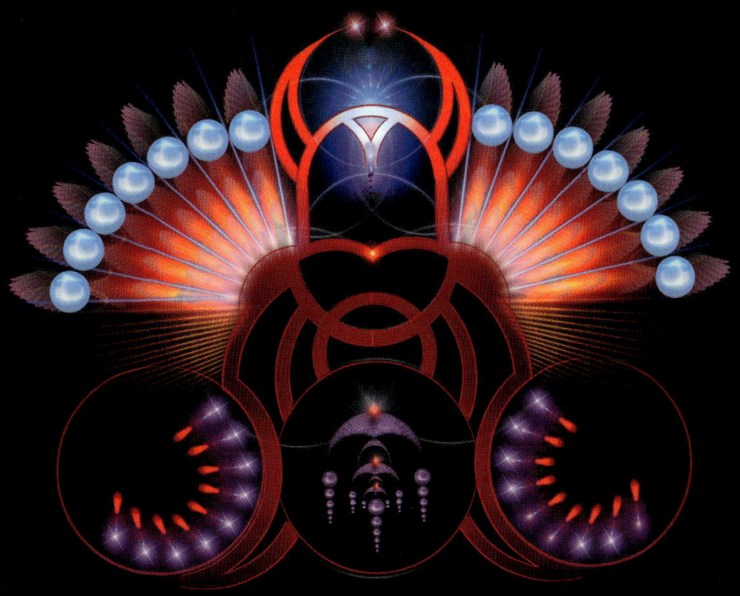

Unconditional love XII

Self-esteem

inner space

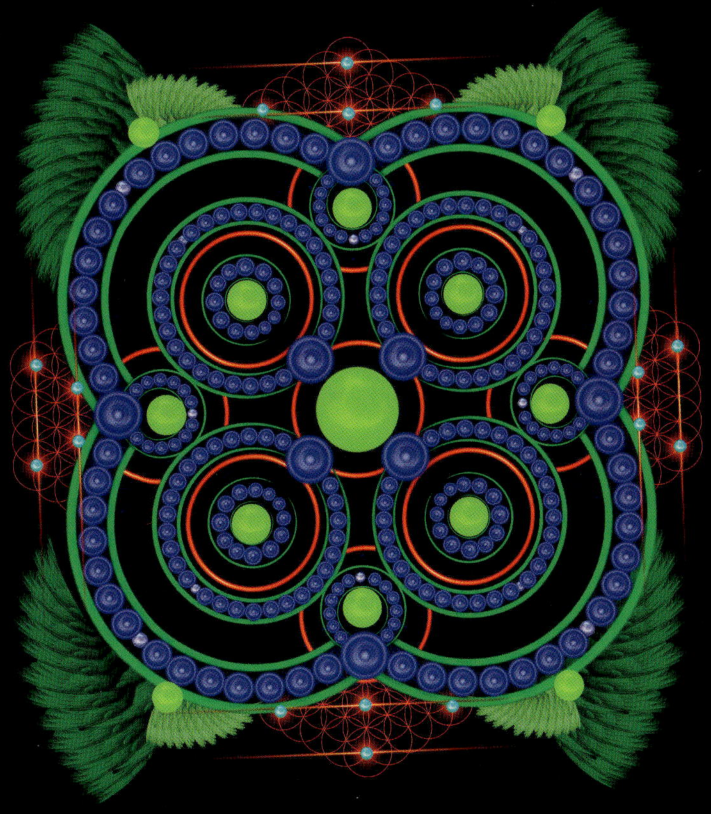

Unconditional love XIII

Intuition

inner space

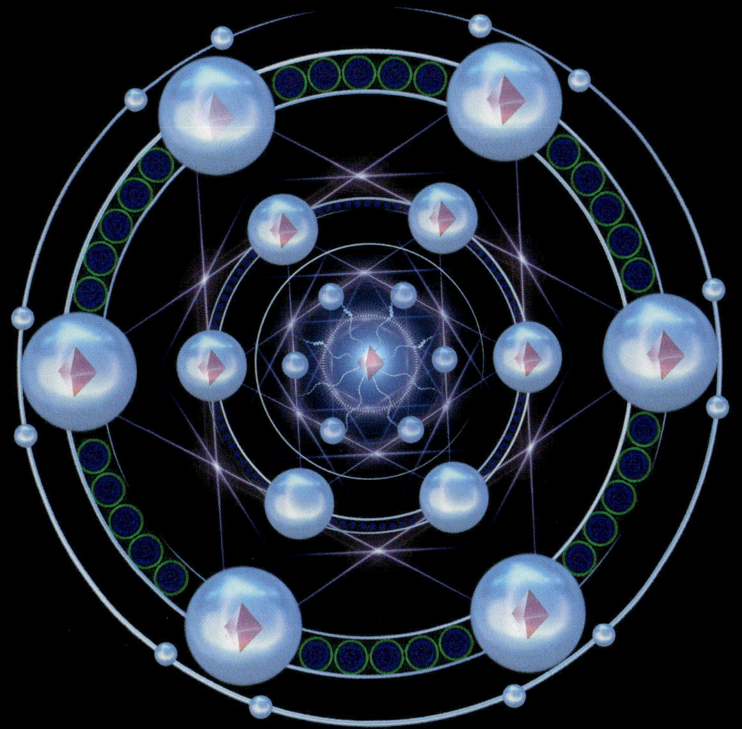

Unconditional love XIV
Blueprint

inner space

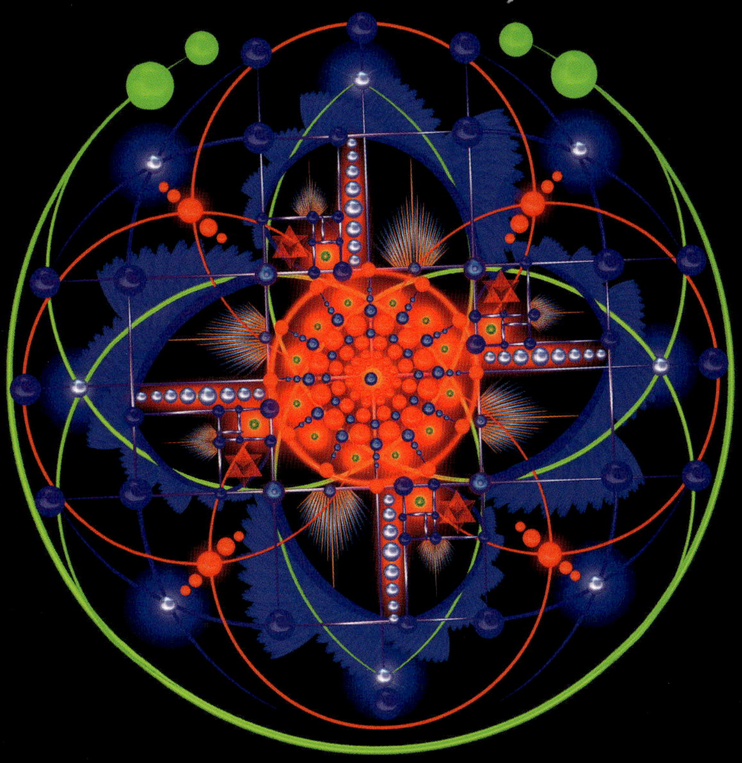

From ego to authenticity I

Authenticity

inner space

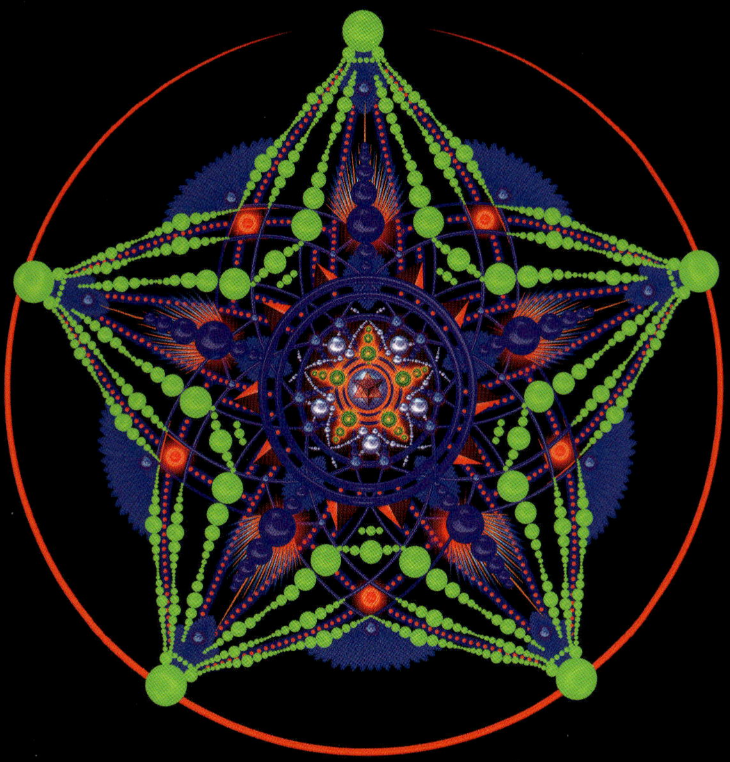

From ego to authenticity II

Expansion

inner space

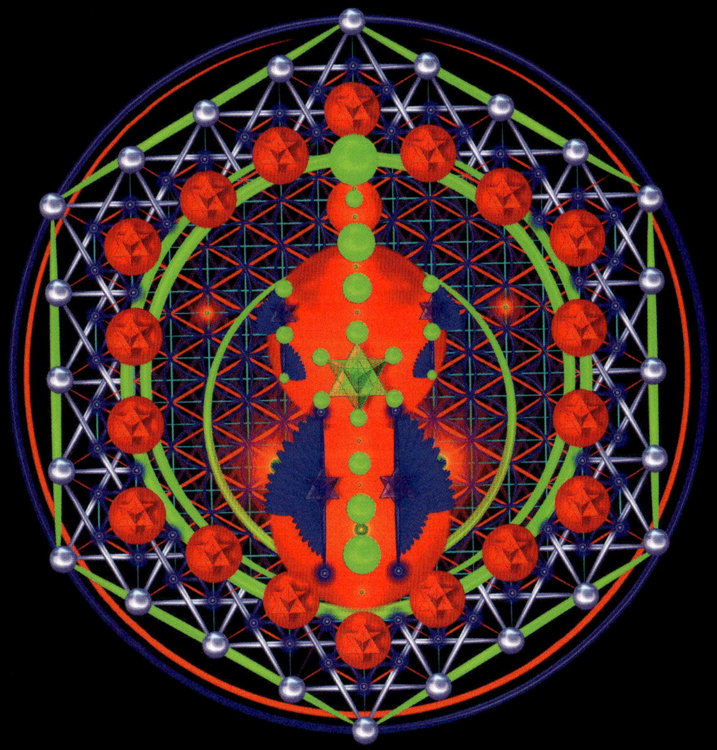

From ego to authenticity III

Rhythm

inner space

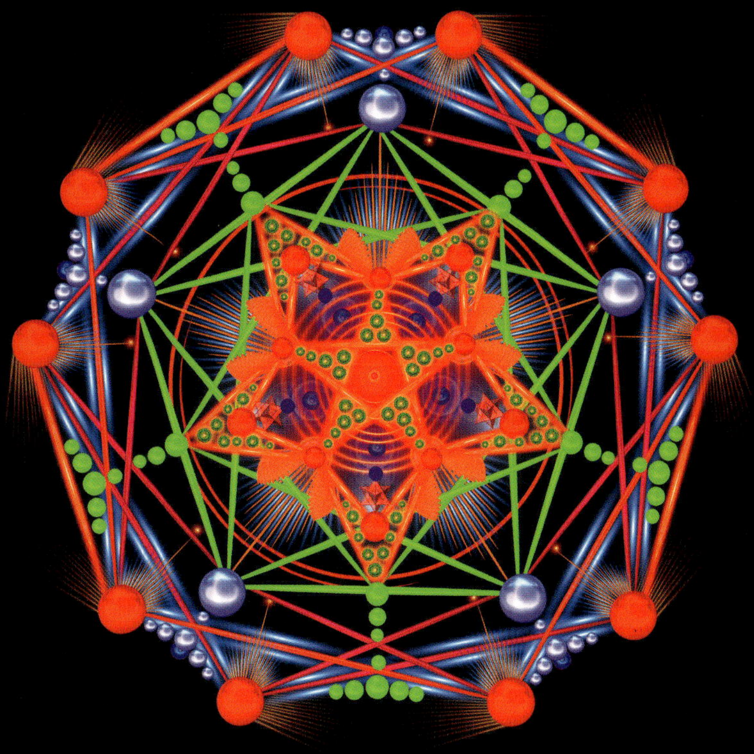

From ego to authenticity IV
Pride

inner space

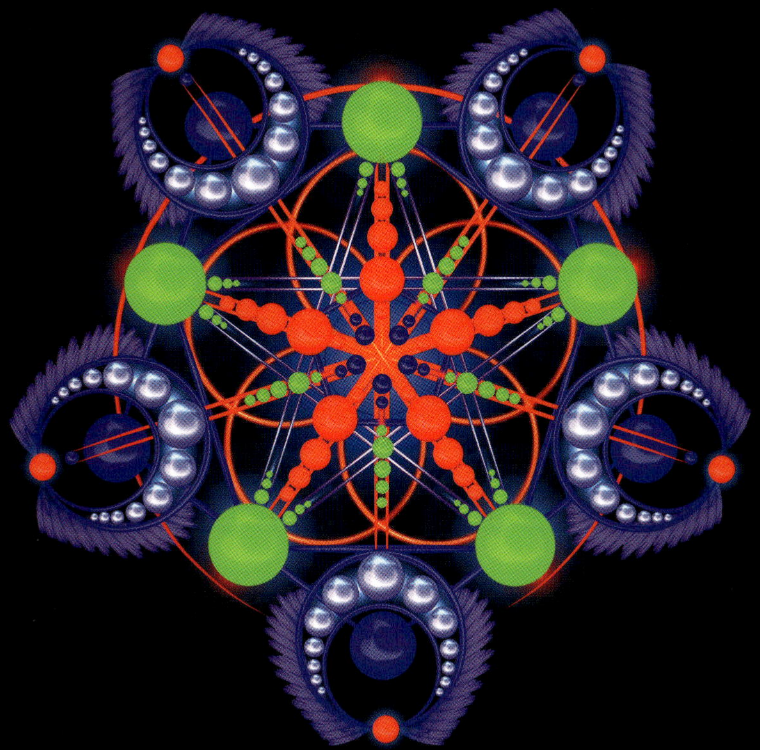

From ego to authenticity V

Vulnerability

inner space

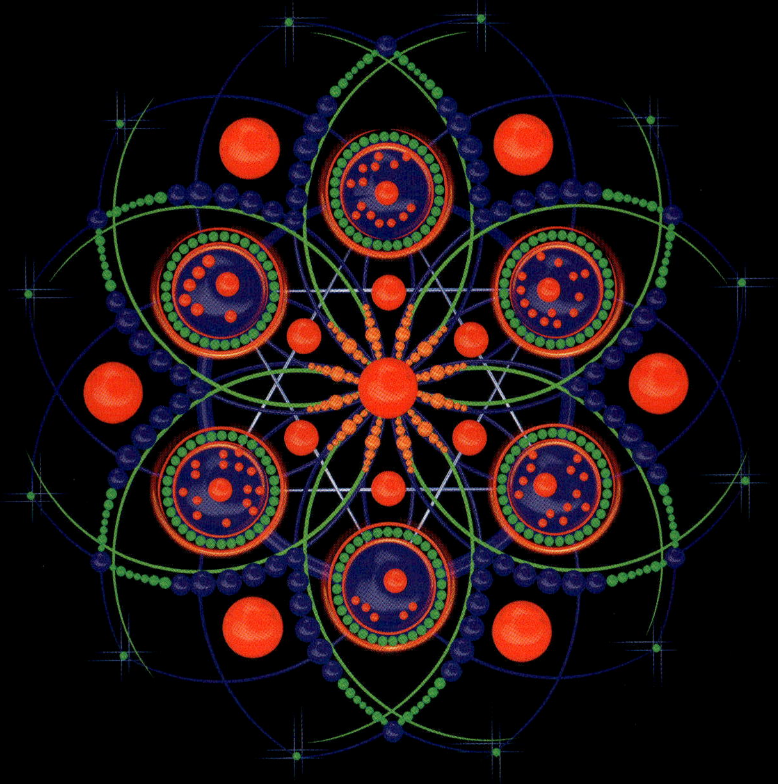

From ego to authenticity VI

Awakening

inner space

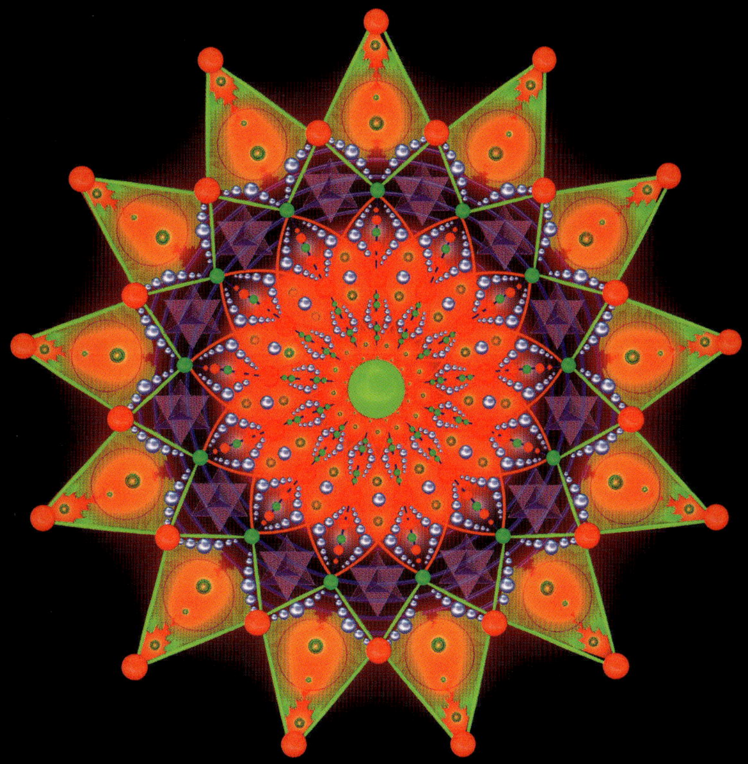

From ego to authenticity VII

Self-healing

inner space

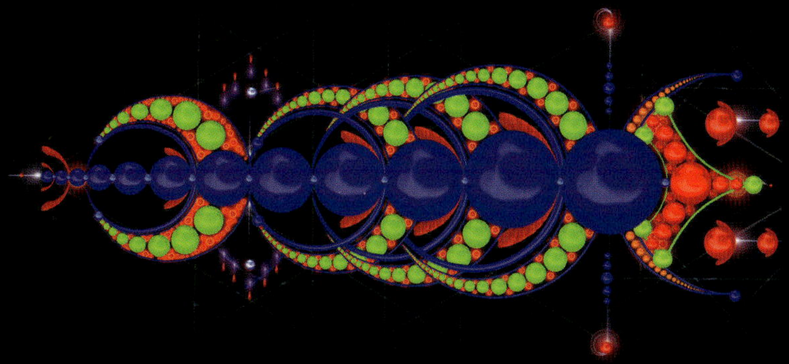

From ego to authenticity VIII
Decisiveness

inner space

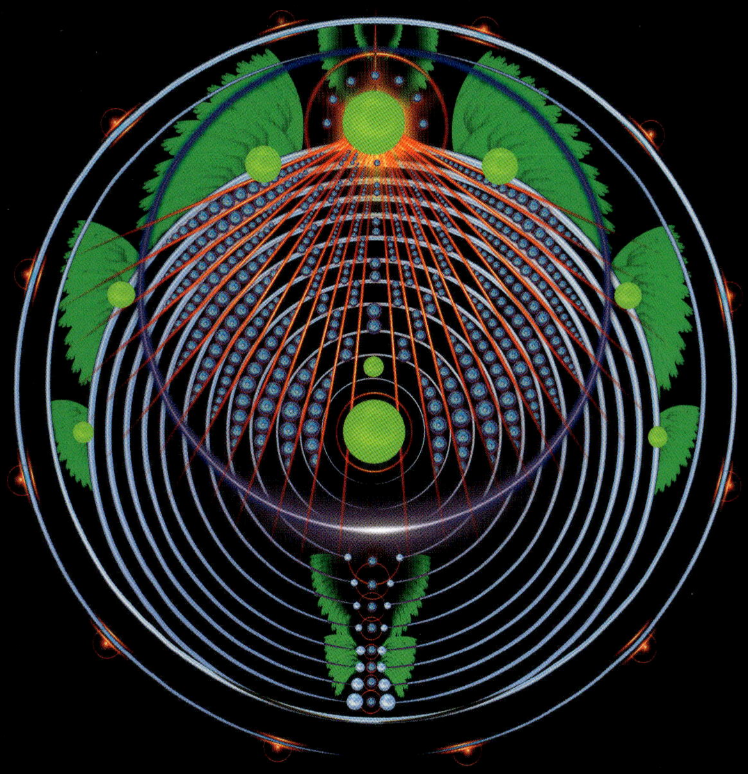

From ego to authenticity IX

Creation

inner space

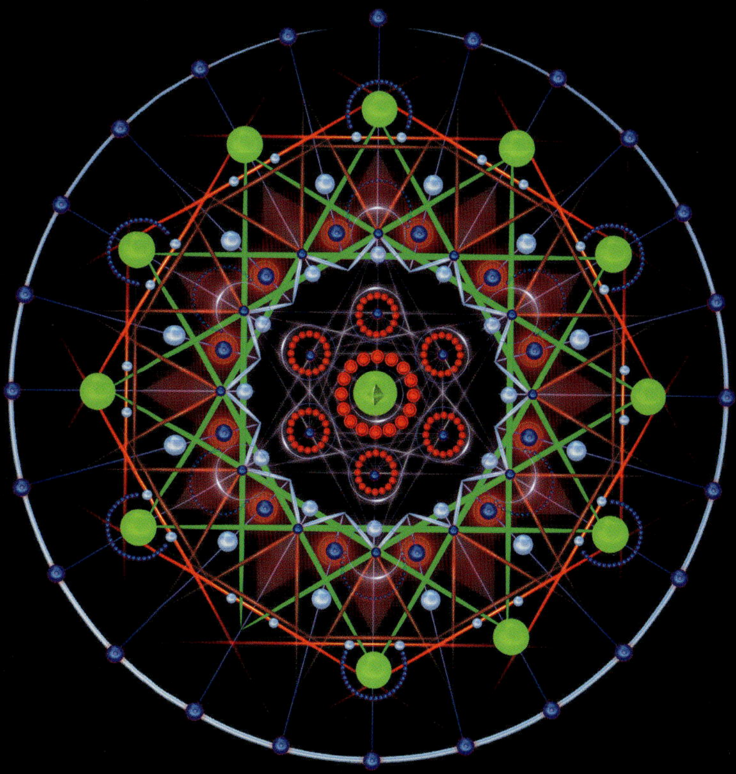

From ego to authenticity X
Synchronicity

inner space

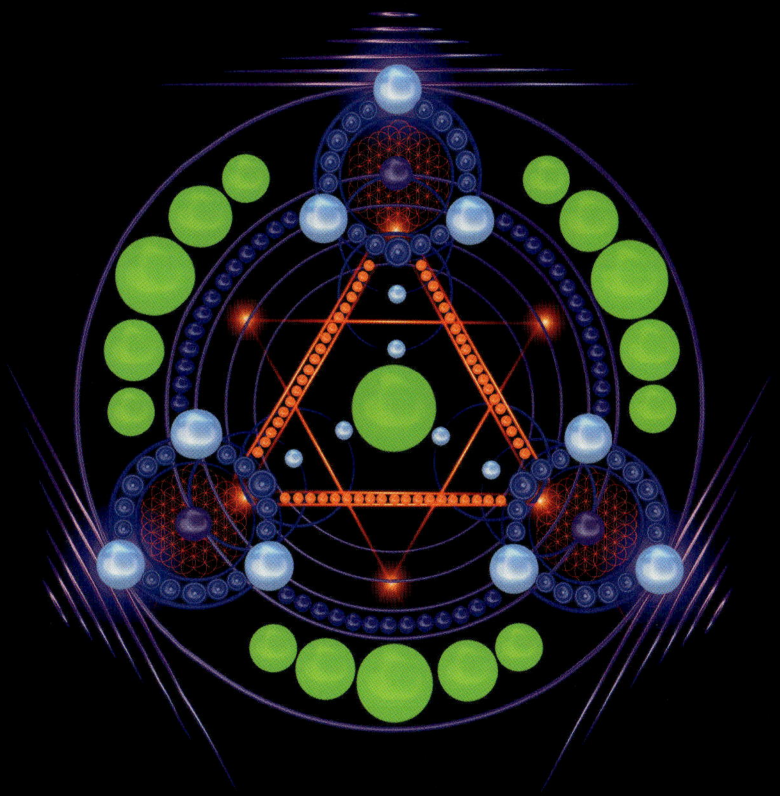

From ego to authenticity XI

Birth

inner space

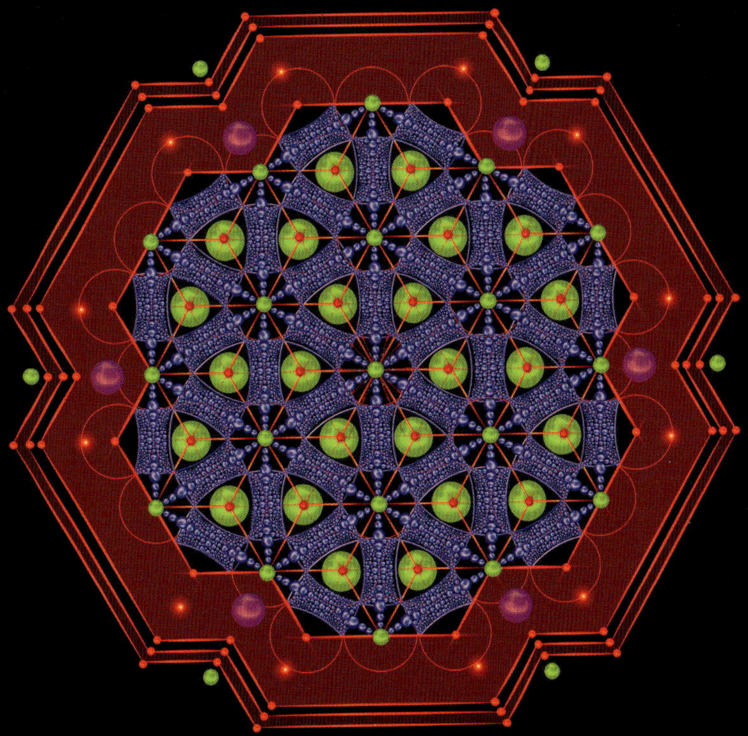

From ego to authenticity XIV

Synergy

inner space

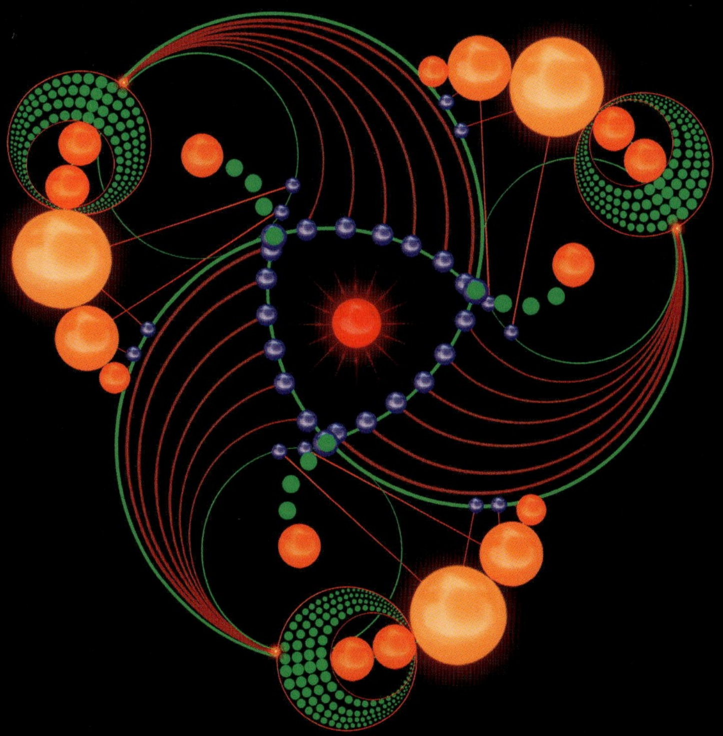

From ego to authenticity XIII

Clarity

inner space

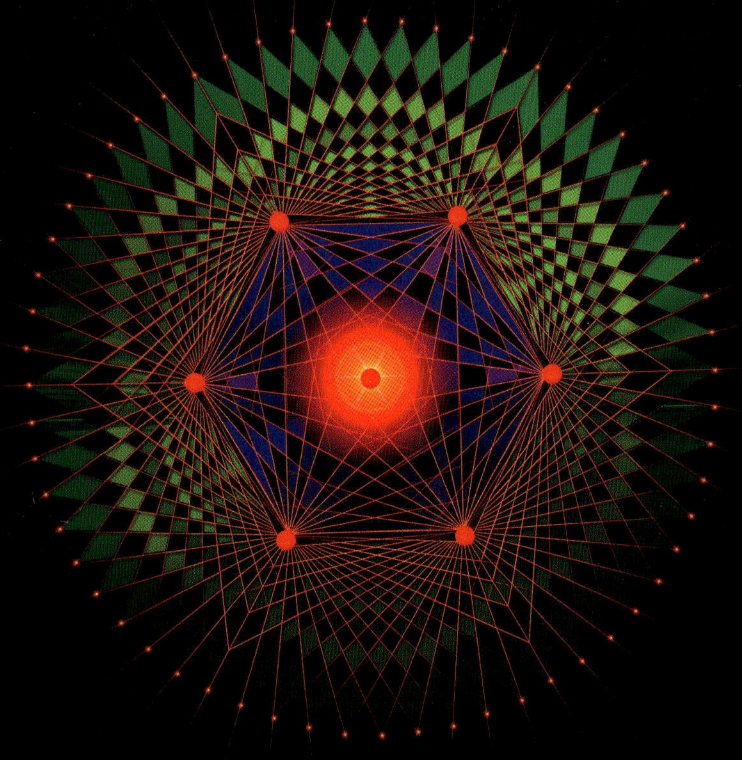

From ego to authenticity XII

Turning point